Teaching with Computers

Computers

A New Menu for the '90s

Mary Jo Langhorne,
Jean O. Donham,
June F. Gross,
and Denise Rehmke

ORYX PRESS

Teaching with Computers

Computers

A New Menu for the '90s

by Mary Jo Langhorne,
Jean O. Donham,
June F. Gross,
and Denise Rehmke

ORYX PRESS
1989

The rare Arabian Oryx is believed to have inspired the myth of the unicorn. This desert antelope became virtually extinct in the early 1960s. At that time several groups of international conservationists arranged to have 9 animals sent to the Phoenix Zoo to be the nucleus of a captive breeding herd. Today the Oryx population is nearly 800, and over 400 have been returned to reserves in the Middle East.

Library of Congress Cataloging-in-Publication Data

Teaching with computers: a new menu for the '90s / by
  Mary Jo Langhorne . . . [et al.].
      p.   cm.
  Bibliography: p.
  Includes index.
  ISBN 0-89774-481-0
    1. Computer-assisted instruction—United States.   I. Langhorne.
  Mary Jo.
  LB1028.5.T385 1989   88-38095
  371.3'9445—dc19   CIP
                                                                      (Rev.)

Dedicated to Robert Moon van Deusen, an exemplary
computer-using educator

Contents

Acknowledgments

The authors acknowledge the following people for their assistance and support: Cheryl Adam, Rollin Bannow, Dan Griffith, John Gross, Dave Hallas, Chuck Kreeb, Carl Jens, Jeanne Jones, Pam Kautz, Jack Kennedy, John Langhorne, Jyl Langhorne, Nan Mercier, Norb Meyer, Jim Remley, Dennis St. John, Donna Trolliet, and Frank Ward.

Preface

No longer an infant technology, computers are in evidence in nearly every school in America. Recent statistics show that nearly 2 million computers have been purchased by schools with the average district owning one computer for every 38 students.

In spite of the large amount of hardware in schools, however, it is now apparent that computers are not a cure-all for educational ills. Many unresolved questions plague those educators charged with planning for computer usage in the schools. What is the best way to use computers? Should we require computer classes? Is it necessary to know programming to be "computer literate"? How shall we deal with ethical questions involving computer use? How can teachers best learn to use computers effectively? What can we do *better* with computers? Too often, these questions have interfered with effective integration of computers into the school program.

The second decade of instructional computing is beginning; it is clearly a time for decision making. In many cases, that decision making has never occurred; computers arrived on the scene so rapidly that there *was* no time for planning. Those responsible for computing in the schools—teachers, administrators, media specialists—must choose from the smorgasbord of computer applications in education those uses that are best-suited to the needs of the local instructional program. The computer is not the curriculum; the computer should not drive the curriculum. Rather, it is a tool which, used properly, can greatly enhance the curriculum.

We have reached a time when it is becoming clear that—as with any new technology—the computer is best used if it provides us with easier or better ways of doing those things which we are already required to do. This is the way computers are treated in the "real world" of business and industry. Students whose future jobs will involve the daily use of computers can best be taught about computers by using them in a variety of ways as a regular part of their school life. This book will describe strategies for integrating computers into the instructional program in ways that have proved to be appropriate and successful.

In Part I, "Planning and Organization," goals for the computer program at both the district and building level are described. Software selection and the management of both hardware and software are detailed, and the question of computer literacy is addressed.

Part II, "Computers in the Curriculum," details successful uses of computers within the instructional program. Areas of emphasis include introductory computer experiences in elementary schools, the use of word processing in the teaching of writing, and the integration of computers into the various subject areas in secondary schools. Using computers to teach high-order thinking skills is described, and a series of lessons designed to teach students to use databases is outlined.

In Part III, "Final Considerations," computer applications that assist administrators and teachers with the preparation of materials and record keeping are discussed. Emerging technologies and issues in instructional computing are also addressed.

Part I
Planning and Organization

Chapter 1
The Phases of Instructional Computing: Literacy through Integration

The use of computers in education is not the compelling issue it was five—or even two—years ago. New bandwagons have presented themselves: Higher-order thinking skills, merit-pay plans, and objective-based education now compete for the attention and funding computers received but a short time ago.

This is a time of evaluation and reassessment in the area of instructional computing. It is a time for decision makers to examine carefully the uses being made of computers in our schools, and ask if those uses are indeed giving us the best return on our investment. It is a time for planners to look at programs and decide where the computer has the greatest potential to effect positive results. It is a time to begin buying hardware and software based on program requirements. In short, it is a time for the tail to stop wagging the dog, for technology to stop determining program, and for us to begin regarding the computer as simply another tool—albeit a powerful one—that can make a difference in our educational programs.

This is not a book about how computers work or the advantages of one operating system over another. This is not a book about computer programming. Nor is it a book that makes extravagant claims about the potential—at least in the immediate future—for computers to totally reform the delivery of instruction. Rather, the authors will provide teachers, administrators, media specialists, and other decision makers with models of successful practices currently in place which *have* improved instruction in many areas. From among these models, and others which appear regularly in computing and education journals, administrators and teachers must choose those that are consistent with the philosophy and goals of the individual district or school, and incorporate them into a systematic plan for the utilization of computer resources in their own particular setting.

As we prepare for the second decade of computers in our schools, it is useful to look back upon where we have been. Schools appear to go through three distinct phases in working toward the goal of integrating computer technology (see Figure 1.1—inspired by Sheila Cory).

FIGURE 1.1. Growing Toward Integration: A Three-Phase Model of Instructional Computing

PHASE	PLACE OF COMPUTER IN INSTRUCTION	PROGRAM PLANNING	SOFTWARE	HARDWARE	STAFF DEVELOPMENT
PHASE 1: GETTING ON THE BANDWAGON	Used as a novelty Computer seen as object of study, programming emphasis.	Limited to decisions on what hardware to purchase.	Very little available MECC, teacher-written, public domain software used.	Acquisition of hardware is primary focus Emphasis on quantity.	Nonexistent Interested teachers learn on their own.
PHASE 2: THE SHOTGUN APPROACH	Used for drill and practice, simulations, educational games. Some applications. Separate computer literacy courses taught.	Some central coordination exists; software evaluation seen as important.	Software purchase increases; single copies of a variety of programs purchased.	Begin to buy hardware-- especially peripherals-- based on need. Coordination of hardware purchase begins.	Generic inservice provided; attendance is voluntary. Some teachers begin to use applications software.
PERIOD OF EVALUATION AND REASSESSMENT OF PRIORITIES					
PHASE 3: PLANFUL INTEGRATION	Computer used when it is most appropriate medium for instruction. Computer literacy occurs through regular, varied use.	District planning emphasizes instructional soundness. Similar building-level planning exists. Evaluation occurs.	Purchase of software based on planning. Multiple copies, lab packs purchased. Formative evaluation provided for.	Computers purchased for specific levels and applications.	Inservice geared to specific teaching needs; participation required.

PHASE 1: GETTING ON THE BANDWAGON

When the affordable microcomputer first appeared some 10 years ago, it was heralded as a vehicle for transforming education. The literature was replete with visions of students seated in front of computers completing individually tailored learning programs or discovering important science and math principles through interaction with the computer. The public quickly caught hold of this vision, and school officials responded to pressure to provide students with the opportunity to learn with computers by purchasing computer hardware in such quantity that by the late 1980s nearly 2 million computers were housed in American schools. Unfortunately, the availability of computer hardware in those early years was not matched by an equal quantity and quality of instructional software or by the expertise to use it in instructionally meaningful ways. Since little planning had occurred, and educators trained in computer use were in short supply, many districts found themselves in the position of having a large supply of hardware but no way to use it to improve instruction.

The absence of quality software and our early naiveté about instructional computing supported the idea advanced by those with some training in computer science that teachers and students would have to learn programming in order to fully realize the potential of the technology. Computer programming classes were offered for both teachers and students. Most teachers soon realized that programming a lesson was too time-consuming to be practical. Consequently, some decided that computers were simply not going to be a useful tool for their teaching.

Student classes in computer programming were more successful. Offering or requiring classes in programming was a tidy, administratively efficient means of demonstrating to a demanding public that the schools were teaching students to use computers. Proponents of programming also pointed to potential gains in such problem-solving skills as sequential planning, precision in defining a problem, and the ability to break large tasks into smaller parts as further justification for teaching programming. Bright students, especially those gifted in mathematics, readily elected programming classes, which gave them frequent access to computers.

As better software was developed, it became clear that students and teachers need not master programming in order to use the technology. Equity questions, particularly male/female ratios in programming classes, made educators eager to explore other applications. Today, enrollments in programming classes are declining, and research findings cast doubt on the claim that programming improves problem-solving ability (Greer 1986; Jansson, Williams and Collins 1987).

Also during this first phase, many schools used early versions of MECC (Minnesota Educational Computing Consortium) or other teacher-written software as a novel way of reinforcing classroom instruction. Such programs tended to be drill-and-practice exercises or educational games with simple graphics and limited sophistication. While teachers observed that such programs were highly motivational, it was difficult to see that any significant instructional gains were occurring. As Phase 1 came to an end, the attitude of many educators was one of ambivalence, and a fair number were convinced that the computer was a passing fancy destined to be sent to storage with the language labs and programmed learning texts.

PHASE 2: THE SHOTGUN APPROACH

The second phase of instructional computing, once described as "the shotgun approach" (Cory 1983), is the one in which most districts find themselves today. It is characterized by a period of exploring many different avenues for computer use. Teachers have been given generic computer training in how to load and use programs, how to turn the machine on and off, and how to care for diskettes, and they have been informed about types of software available. A variety of software has been purchased and is used in many areas. Usually, the allocation of computers is determined by which teachers are most enthusiastic about computer use. Breadth, not depth, is the rule, and teachers may feel pressured to incorporate computers into their teaching.

In an effort to provide exposure to computers for all students, a computer literacy class may be required. Such a class includes information on the history of computers and their place in society, some programming instruction, keyboarding, and an introduction to applications such as word processing and databases.

As the purchase of software increases during Phase 2, and the demand grows for peripherals such as printers, memory upgrades, and extra disk drives, the need for central coordination becomes evident. A district committee may be formed to examine issues such as criteria for purchasing hardware and software, the need for better training for teachers, and areas in which certain applications can most beneficially be taught. As such planning occurs, the computer begins to be regarded as a tool for instruction, rather than as an object of instruction or a mere novelty.

PHASE 3: PLANFUL INTEGRATION

Once central planning at both the district and building level begins to occur, decision makers realize that computer resources can be stretched only so far. This is the time to evaluate existing uses of the computer, and it can be a difficult one. Computer resources can no longer be allocated on the basis of which teacher is most enthusiastic or to provide something for students to do after they have completed regular work in the classroom. Planning must be based upon instructional priorities already in place, and must include careful consideration of the questions, "Will the computer enable us to teach this content or process better?" and "Will the computer enable us to teach something we could not teach before?" If, in examining a building's priorities, the improvement of student writing is found to be a goal, the teaching of word processing may become the best use of that building's computer resources since it enables students to complete the editing and revision cycle involved in writing in a better way than is possible without word processing. If modernizing a high school class in industrial technology is a goal, the purchase of equipment and software suitable for computer-aided drafting becomes a priority since it enables us to teach in a way that was not possible before.

In Phase 3, hardware and software decisions are made only after program goals have been established. If a high school has a strong commitment to computerizing its business education program, the hardware and software chosen should be similar to that used for real-world business applications. If teaching problem solving using commercial software developed for that purpose is a goal, schools must buy computers for which such software has been developed. If computer-aided instruction in a lab setting is a priority, a commitment to buying multiple copies or "lab packs" of suitable software is essential. Once such priorities have been established, teachers must be provided with inservice training that is specifically geared to these priorities. While in Phase 2 there is an attempt to do as many things as possible with computers, in Phase 3 the emphasis may be on doing fewer things, but doing them very well. A Phase 3 program is characterized by careful planning and a commitment to training.

Before most schools can attain a Phase 3 program, a period of evaluation and reassignment of computer resources must occur. Decision makers will need to examine practices already in place and determine whether they make the best use of existing computers. Such reassessment may be painful. If it is determined that massing computers in a lab setting for word processing instruction is a higher priority, teachers who have had computers assigned to their rooms for individual drill and practice must be asked to surrender those machines. The instructor whose assignment has been to teach computer literacy and programming classes may need to be reassigned as those areas are integrated into the curriculum. Computers have entered our schools at a pace unmatched by any other new technology; contrast the slow assimilation of video into instruction with that of computers. When they arrived, computers were largely unplanned for and their potential was misunderstood. We know now that computers are here to stay and that their impact on education will be significant. The challenge for the next decade is to see that computers are used in ways that will maximize that impact.

WHAT ABOUT COMPUTER LITERACY?

No book on computers in education would be complete without a discussion of the question "What is computer literacy?" Surely, it is a goal of every school program to prepare students to live in a society where computers will affect nearly every area of life, and where an estimated 75 percent of all jobs will involve computers in some way (Naisbitt 1982).

Computer literacy might be conceptualized as having three components: knowledge about computers, knowledge of computer applications, and knowledge about social issues pertaining to computers (see Figure 1.2).

Knowledge about Computers

Knowledge about computers consists of basic instruction in the operation of a computer and how it works. Students must know what the components of a system are, how to turn the computer on and off, and how to load a program from a menu. Some instruction in basic keyboarding is necessary, and students should have a general understanding of how a computer program works. These skills can best be taught as students are required to use the computer to achieve various instructional goals. The first time a student is required to use a computer in elementary school is the appropriate time to teach basic operations. Keyboarding instruction logically precedes the introduction of word processing. Math class is the obvious area in which to give students a general understanding of the step-by-step sequence a computer follows in running a program.

Knowledge of Applications

Knowledge of applications refers to software and hardware designed to perform some specific job. The most common application in schools today is word processing. The use of databases and spreadsheets to manage and manipulate information is of obvious importance in our information-rich world. Other applications include the use of hardware such as robots or graphics tablets operated by computer. These applications are all examples of real-life uses of computer technology. As the student uses them in a variety of subject areas, he or she gains an understanding of the capabilities, and the limitations, of computer technology.

Social Issues Related to Computers

The third component of computer literacy is an understanding of the social issues related to computers. Promoting the ethical use of computers both on the personal level of conforming to copyright regulations and on the more global level of ensuring individual privacy must be of concern to us all. The impact of computer technology as we move from the industrial age to the information age, the implications of rapid change, and the need for students to be prepared for frequent job retraining during their lifetime must be addressed. The obvious place for discussion of these issues is within the social science curriculum.

FIGURE 1.2. Computer Literacy: An Integrated Approach

Competency	Components	Where Taught
1. Knowledge about Computers	Basic operation • on/off • loading/using software • disk care • disk and file procedures	Taught where computers are first encountered in curriculum. Reinforced frequently as students use computers.
	Keyboarding	Precedes teaching of word processing; late elementary. Reinforced whenever word processing is used
	Use of printer	As needed for word processing
	Understanding of how a program works.	Middle grades; when thinking and math skills are developed.
2. Knowledge of Applications	Word processing	Language Arts- late elementary or early Junior High.
	Databases	Junior/Senior High - Social Studies, Science, Business Ed.
	Spreadsheets	Senior High - Business, Math, Economics
	Graphic Arts - Drawing, Drafting, Desktop Publishing	Junior/Senior High-Art, Journalism, Business, Industrial Technology
	Robotics	Junior/Senior High-Science, Industrial Technology
	Electronic Music	Junior/Senior High-Music
	Computer-Assisted Instruction	Where appropriate
3. Knowledge about Social Issues Related to Computers	Copyright law	When computers are first used; reinforced at every level
	Right to privacy	Social studies classes
	Impact of technology on future life	Social studies, Science, Career education
	Information age awareness	Library media classes, Social studies

Computer literacy becomes a by-product of Phase 3 with its emphasis on planned integration. As the applications and issues dealt with in computer literacy classes are absorbed into areas of the curriculum where they fit naturally, there no longer exists a need for separate classes in computer literacy. Students become computer literate by using computers in a variety of ways as a part of the regular school program. It must be emphasized, however, that thoughtful planning is essential if computer literacy is to be achieved in this way. Care must be taken that *all* students are exposed to essential computer skills in a sequential and systematic way.

SUMMARY

There are three distinct phases in implementing instructional computing in the schools. In the first phase, emphasis is primarily on the acquisition of hardware. Most schools have moved beyond this into a second phase where computers are used in as many areas as possible, often without attention to appropriateness. As a result of planning and establishing priorities, schools can move to Phase 3, in which computers are integrated into instruction in ways that maximize the impact of computer technology on education and produce computer-competent graduates.

The intent of this book is to help those responsible for planning and implementing district- and building-level programs in instructional computing make decisions relating to how computers should be used. Making these decisions is only the beginning. Integrating computers into the instructional program requires a strong commitment to training, since teaching with a computer is unlike teaching with any other technology. The following chapters will provide guidelines for planning at both district and building levels, a model for selecting software to fit curriculum, and a plan for inservice that will enable teachers to accomplish the goal of integration. The intent of this book is to help educators reach Phase 3 in instructional computing.

REFERENCES

Cory, Sheila. "A Four-Stage Model of Development for Full Implementation of Computers for Instruction." *The Computing Teacher* 10 (November 1983): 11–16.

Greer, Jim. "High School Experience and University Achievement in Computer Science." *A.E.D.S. Journal* 19 (Winter/Spring 1986): 216–25.

Jansson, Lars C., Harvey D. Williams and Robert J. Collins. "Computer Programming and Mathematics." *School Science and Mathematics* 87 (May 1987): 371–79.

Naisbitt, John. *Megatrends.* New York: Warner Books, 1982.

Chapter 2
The District Plan

In content areas like reading, mathematics, or social studies, careful planning and articulation are critical. So too is the development of a comprehensive plan for instructional computing. A district must commit both money and personnel to integrate computing into the curriculum. This makes district-level planning particularly important. Front-end planning is the ideal. But many districts find themselves midstream and in need of revising or realigning their computer plan or direction. Either way, some critical elements must be present in the planning process. First, the value of a coordinated, articulated plan must be recognized at all levels.

Vision is a critical element of the district plan. There must be insight into how computer technology fits into the rest of the district's program. Foresight is an important component of vision. While no one can predict the future, district-level leadership must take a critical look at past and present educational practices, as well as the realistic potential for microcomputer technology. Technological projections are particularly difficult because technology changes rapidly. However, if one not only places credence in technological potential but also looks carefully at the human resources of schools, the development of a realistic vision is possible. There appear in the literature images of "high-tech" classrooms or students learning at home via modem. However, the vision needs to include the social aspects of schooling in America and the conservative degree of change in the past hundred years. Then, a vision of assimilating microcomputer technology into a familiar-looking school is more likely. The vision must take all factors into account—social, traditional, economic, and academic. Such a vision suggests, then, a planning process which assumes that many aspects of American schools will not change. Leaders must then say, "What can we do with this technology to improve our current delivery of instruction?"

Leadership in the development of a district plan for instructional computing is critical. Where that leadership emerges can make a difference in the direction the district plan takes. In many school districts, leadership has emerged from the mathematics department, where computer programming has been identified as an important aspect of the district plan. The result has been the development of a program that revolves around the mathematics department with considerable emphasis on a computer science curriculum and minimal consideration for other computer applications. In some districts, the leadership has come from the business education department; in those instances the emphasis has been on business applications. Students enrolled in a business elective program have access to courses in word processing, database management, and spreadsheets. If leadership based in a specific department can identify significant and appropriate computer applications across disciplines, then the source of the leadership may not be critical. However, if the leadership comes from a specific department and that department becomes the only or primary computing department, then the leadership is too narrow in its focus.

A less frequent but highly appropriate place for leadership to emerge is the media department. By its nature, the media department is interdisciplinary. Media departments perceive themselves as responding to all departments. The potential for a comprehensive plan exists if the leadership for district-level planning comes from this interdisciplinary source where the concerns of mathematics, business, language arts, science, social studies, industrial arts, information science, and all other departments have equal consideration. Media professionals have a view of curriculum which teachers in specific departments or grade levels cannot have. It is the business of media to know the curriculum and to see its articulation across the board. Furthermore, the development of instructional uses of new technologies is clearly within a media department's purview. A case can be made for combining district-level computing coordination and media coordination based on the issue of equity across disciplines; furthermore, it is the media professional whose literature addresses educational technology. Indeed, the computer is often perceived as another instructional medium. Thus a district may do well to look to this professional specialty for district-level leadership.

Ownership of the district-level planning process must be shared among representatives of several concerned groups. District-level planning should be led by a central office professional who can address the issues of instructional computing across disciplines. The planning process must involve a committee of teachers and administrators from the district. Various levels and content areas should be represented; elementary and secondary classroom teachers, media specialists, and curriculum coordinators are examples of positions to be represented on the committee. Another potential member of the committee is the district's business manager, since there are significant fiscal issues to be addressed. However, this must be a working committee; membership of more than 15 can become too cumbersome to be productive. In addition to educators on the committee, advisory members from the community should be considered; these might include members of the business community, higher education, or parent groups. The value of having such members serve on the committee includes a sense of community ownership of the plan as well as an increased level of awareness among community members. Such members bring a perspective to the planning process that might otherwise be overlooked. Business people may have suggestions for high school business application electives. Parents may have concerns about expectations for word-processed papers and the pressure for home computers. The broader the base of ownership of the planning process, the greater the commitment in energy to implement and in resources to facilitate.

No plan related to technology can ever be considered finished. Continual change in the capabilities of the technology demands continual review of the plan. Moreover, because of the newness, errors are bound to be made. Progress, impact, and attitude must be reviewed continually to catch errors and to correct courses of development. There has been no existing blueprint for instructional computing.

The planning process ought not to be a "start-from-scratch" process in any district. There should be networks of similar districts where exchange of successes and failures can occur. Moreover, the vast array of instructional computing periodicals should provide a rich resource of ideas which worked or didn't work. A planning committee should be tapping that resource regularly. Using consultants from universities, business, and other school districts is yet another way to gather information to make reasoned decisions.

District plans for instructional computing are more than a scope and sequence of computer skills. There are several important components of a district plan:

- Philosophy
- Applications
- Software
- Hardware
- Funding
- Inservice
- Evaluation

The relationships among these components are depicted in Figure 2.1. The planning process begins with the development of a philosophy of instructional computing. Once that philosophy is agreed upon, then appropriate instructional computing applications can be identified based on the philosophy. Applications will lead to an investigation of software to determine what will best facilitate the applications identified as valid for the individual district. Software

FIGURE 2.1. Components of a District Plan

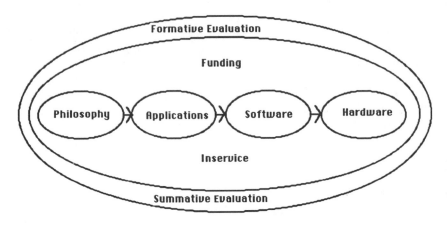

will govern what hardware will be appropriate. This process must occur in an environment in which funding will be available to implement the plan. Another factor that must be available in the environment is inservice; throughout the planning process, leaders must be able to assume the availability of inservice providers, staff time to attend inservice, and support for acclimation to change. Surrounding the process should be frequent formative evaluation to help in slight course corrections and periodic summative evaluation to gather data on impact.

PHILOSOPHY

The planning process begins with development of a philosophy related to instructional computing. Moreover, that philosophy and all decisions related to instructional uses of computers must be consistent with the educational philosophy already in place in a district. For example, in a district where the authoring cycle is firmly in place as a philosophy in the teaching of writing, word processing clearly has a place. It ought to be placed at the grade level where revision becomes an important step in the authoring cycle, since revision is the power of the word processor. In a district where a holistic approach to the teaching of reading and writing is the philosophy, drill-and-practice programs on phonetic approaches to reading should be considered with skepticism, as they do not fit the instructional philosophy. In a district where kindergarten math and science concepts are taught concretely with physical manipulatives, it hardly seems appropriate to place computers in the kindergarten room for teaching math and science concepts in the semiabstract.

If the microcomputer is seen as an instructional tool, then the development of a separate computer curriculum is inappropriate. Instead, the use of this instructional tool should be integrated into the existing curriculum. If another component of that philosophy is that computers are not a panacea for all content and all students, then cramming computer-related instruction into every content area and expecting every teacher to be a computing teacher is not appropriate. What must occur in the planning process, then, is a development of a list of "This we believe" statements. These statements must be the guiding principles of that planning process. Consistency between the instructional computing philosophy and the educational philosophy is essential.

APPLICATIONS

Determining appropriate applications at each level or in each department is an important part of the district-level planning task. These decisions must take into account philosophy of both instructional computing and pedagogy. Two general questions must be addressed in identifying which computer applications should be undertaken by a district: "Will the computer allow me to teach something better, faster, and more efficiently?" and "Will the computer allow me to teach concepts that I could not teach otherwise?" Often there is a tendency to choose to do something via computer because it is possible, not because it is best. Given the limited resources of schools, it makes sense to choose to use the computer when it is best, not just possible. A striking example is the decision to drill math facts on the computer. Clearly, flash cards have been serving this purpose very well for many years in schools. Even with the best of drill-and-practice software, a student is likely to spend fewer actual minutes practicing the facts at the computer than he or she would spend in actual drill with flash cards. Furthermore, several sets of flash cards can be used, quite economically, at one time in a classroom, as compared with the cost of several computers. Indeed, a recent study comparing computer-based and flash card drill showed no significant difference in achievement over a six-week period of daily practice in math facts (Fuson and Brinko 1985). On the other hand, students can organize information on a database management program to make comparisons and draw inferences based on those comparisons. This could not be accomplished without a computerized database management program. This application clearly becomes a better place to spend a school's resources.

Identifying a limited number of applications is a key decision. A common pitfall for planners is to attempt to use the computer for too many applications. A district's resources—hardware, software, teacher inservice—can be spread so thin that use is superficial. Moreover, less powerful computer applications can limit the potential for important ones. How to limit applications can vary from district to district. One method is to limit grade level involvement. A district could make a case for limiting instructional computer use to students in grades 4 and above. The basis for such a decision might be that the philosophy of the district places heavy emphasis on physical manipulation of concrete objects in concept attainment at primary grade levels. Or a district might say that in writing revision is not as important as fluency at the primary level, so the computer as a word processor is less necessary here than at fourth grade and above where revision is emphasized. "Depth, not breadth" is an appropriate motto.

Figure 2.2 shows an example of one district's identified computer applications, given limitations on hardware, software, and personnel.

FIGURE 2.2. Selected Computer Applications

Level	Application
Grades K-3	• No computer use
Grades 4-6	• Problem-solving skills taught with one computer and a large monitor • Word processing in the authoring cycle
Grades 7-8	• Word processing in language arts and business • Databases in science • Selected CAI in social studies and science
Grades 9-12	• Electives in business applications • Electives in programming • Word processing in language arts • Online bibliographic data base searching in social studies • Computer-aided drafting (CAD) • Desktop publishing • Selected CAI in foreign language • Scientific instrumentation

This example demonstrates the selectivity that should go into identification of applications. The selection of hardware is based directly on the identification of applications. Once those applications are chosen, it becomes possible to determine which equipment will best suit each application and how much of that equipment is needed. For the example described in Figure 2.2, hardware would be allocated as outlined in Figure 2.3. This is only an example; the intent is to emphasize the selectivity in choosing applications and the matching between applications and allocation of resources. This example demonstrates rather limited amounts of equipment and limited uses. It is a plan within the economic reach of many midsize school districts. The intent is to purchase specific equipment for specific applications. More important, the intent is to determine the application first and then purchase equipment to meet that need.

FIGURE 2.3. Sample Hardware Needs for Selected Applications

Level	Hardware
Grades K-3	• No equipment
Grades 4-6	• Computer labs of 12 computers with 3 printers and printer switch boxes to accommodate half a class • Large-screen display device
Grades 7-8	• Computer labs with 28 computers and 7 printers with switch boxes to accommodate a class • Large-screen display device
Grades 9-12	• Computer lab with 16 Leading Edge computers and 4 printers with switch boxes for business education • Computer lab with 12 dual-drive Apple computers and 3 printers with switch boxes for programming class and CAD use • Computer lab with 12 Apple computers and 3 printers with switch boxes for word processing in writing classes • Large-screen monitor • Apple computer and modem equipped with communications software for online searching • Macintosh system for desktop publishing

Early in the instructional computing movement, most districts purchased hardware before anyone knew how to use the technology effectively. Hardware decisions may have been based on the wrong criteria and may not have been associated with specific applications. In such situations, it still makes sense to identify what applications now seem appropriate, assess the capability of available hardware and software to implement these applications, allocate current resources to meet identified program needs and identify what resources are yet needed. From this point, the application decisions can then drive purchase decisions.

SOFTWARE

Selection of software is a major concern at the district level. Software purchase ought to be centrally coordinated to ensure adherence to the district philosophy for computer use, to improve both vertical and horizontal articulation, and to establish quality control.

District-adopted criteria and standards of excellence should be established for software. No software should be purchased before it has been previewed and evaluated against the district's criteria. Classroom teachers should be involved in the preview process. Chapter 4 provides a detailed description of an effective software selection process.

HARDWARE

Equipment purchases represent a substantial part of the cost of instructional computing. Yet it is the software that is critical in developing a program. It makes sense to choose the hardware in part based on the software availability and its match with the applications identified as appropriate for a district.

There is some value in maintaining a degree of equipment consistency across a district for the sake of bulk purchase, software compatibility, and in-house service. Another reason for some consistency is to facilitate teacher inservice across the district. Yet hardware must be evaluated with the application in mind. Total consistency may not be appropriate. Selection of peripherals likewise must match applications and software requirements.

FUNDING

Budget is a critical component of the district plan. If a district is genuinely committed to instructional computing, some amount of district money should be allocated to support it. Many districts are guilty of using Chapter 2 Block Grant monies or contributions from parent groups as the sole source of funding to purchase hardware and software. Their programs are limited to what can be covered by those dollars. Such a budget constitutes no commitment to the program. This type of budgeting for instructional computing is risky at best, considering the tenuous character of Chapter 2 funding and contributions. In addition, contributed dollars often come with strings attached which may influence the use of the money in ways not consistent with the overall plan or philosophy. For example, consider a situation where kindergarten use of computers is inconsistent with philosophy. Parent donations may come with the expectation of access to the computer by all students regardless of appropriateness. Moreover, this is short-sighted budgeting since it does not take into account several other costs that are a part of instructional computing. An instructional computing budget must have provisions for the following:

Hardware: computers (new and replacement)
           printers (new and replacement)
           peripherals
           upgrades
           maintenance and repair

Software purchase

Teacher inservice: presenters
                    substitutes for teacher release
                    materials
                    conference registrations/expenses

Personnel: computer lab aides
            district coordinator
            building-level coordinator
            hardware technician

Supplies: blank diskettes
           printer ribbons
           printer paper
           storage containers

Facilities: electrical upgrades
             remodeling of space
             furniture

A more appropriate funding plan is to establish technology as a line item in the district budget. Perhaps a per-pupil technology allocation is one solution to the funding problem.

INSERVICE

Teachers are at the heart of instructional computing. A district plan must include provision for teacher inservice. A very small percentage of today's teachers have been introduced to instructional computing as a part of their teacher training program. Moreover, much of teacher behavior is the enactment of models teachers have observed. Since the microcomputer is a technology of the 1980s, it is highly unlikely that many of today's teachers learned via microcomputer technology. Therefore, each district must develop an inservice program to support teachers in this new technique. In early efforts at teacher inservice in this area, leaders made a pass at teaching teachers about computers. However, the selection of content was simplistic—not related to the tasks teachers would be doing, but rather someone's idea of computer literacy. Instead, inservice should resemble training programs in business settings, where the content is prescribed for each category of teachers so that it relates directly to the uses they will make of computers in their classrooms. Just as hardware decisions must match application decisions, so inservice decisions must match application decisions.

EVALUATION

Formative evaluation is particularly important in the area of instructional computing. The planning process must include development of instruments for evaluation. Evaluation instruments need to be developed for students, teachers at all levels, and administrators at all levels. All aspects of the plan should be addressed. The results must be analyzed and used by the planning team in revising the district plan. In addition, teachers and administrators should receive information summarizing the findings of the evaluation process. Formal evaluation of this type should occur on a regular cycle; five years has been considered appropriate in that this amount of time allows for teachers to have implemented the plan and for students to have had a sequence of experiences of long enough duration to make a difference.

Besides formal evaluation, continuous, informal assessment of computer-related activities is necessary. The district-level coordinator must observe activities in schools, meet with building-level leaders, meet with classroom teachers, meet with building-level and district-level administrators, and meet with parent groups to gather data on progress and concerns. These kinds of data are essential in making improvements in the plan and its implementation.

A model describing stages of implementation of computers for instruction is discussed in Chapter 1. Such a model can be used as a guide for assessing a district's status as it moves toward full integration. A district can identify at which phase its program is operating and identify changes which need to occur in order to move to the next phase. This type of assessment can help determine categories into which additional resources need to be diverted.

SUMMARY

Long-range, comprehensive planning at the district level provides direction for short-term decisions. Such planning increases the likelihood that resources will be used wisely, that teacher time and energy will be committed appropriately, that students will experience an articulated program, and that the school community will feel a sense of pride and ownership in what is happening in this area. Despite the common claim that long-range planning cannot occur in an area of technology because of rapid change, school districts can indeed establish philosophy and guidelines to aid their decision making. While technological change occurs daily, the changes that actually affect schools occur at a reasonable pace. There is no reason for schools to feel pressured into buying into every new technological advancement that comes along. Some of those advancements will be beneficial to instruction; some will not. Some will fit the district's philosophy; some will not. Districts must assess each critically, asking, "Will this advance allow me to teach concepts which I could not otherwise teach?" or "Will this advance allow me to teach something better, faster, and more efficiently than I now can?"

REFERENCES

Fuson, K. C. and K. T. Brinko. "The Comparative Effectiveness of Microcomputers and Flash Cards in the Drill and Practice of Basic Mathematics Facts." *Journal of Research in Mathematics Education* 16 (September 1985): 225–32.

McIntosh, Christine. "The Need for a Computer/Media Coordinator in a Public School System." *Tech Trends* 32 (October 1987): 16–19.

Mojkowski, Charles. "Technology and Curriculum: Will the Promised Revolution Take Place?" *National Association of Secondary School Principals Bulletin* (February 1987): 113–18.

Chapter 3
Planning for Instructional Computing at the Building Level

If effective planning for instructional computing exists at the district level, building personnel will find their task greatly simplified as they move toward Phase 3 (planful integration). Many decisions regarding program philosophy, hardware and software selection, funding, and the sequence for integrating instructional computing will already have been made. Building-level staff must be included in such district planning so that communication exists between the two levels, and buildings develop a sense of ownership of the plan. As with any program planning, the greater the involvement of those who will be delivering the instruction, the greater the likelihood of success.

Leadership at the building level is critical for effective program implementation. Building leaders must possess a clear vision of the role computers can play in improving instruction and must have the ability to inspire others to join in this vision. A study reported in *School Tech News* (1987), identified several critical elements of a successful building program. One such element is a "key 'mover and shaker,'" who is a person respected by the faculty and capable of getting things done. There are several other attributes of an effective building computer coordinator. A thorough knowledge of the school's curriculum is essential in order for instructional computing to be integrated into areas where it is likely to produce the best results. A building coordinator must be someone who is organized and competent at managing resources—computer hardware and software—in a flexible and productive way. This person must be an initiator, but one who pursues goals in a nonthreatening way, and who can provide support for staff who feel uncomfortable about working with computers.

Some schools have hired building-level computer coordinators to direct the development of the school's program. This person may have additional responsibilities, including the teaching of computing classes. If strong leadership exists at the district level, it is doubtful that a full-time professional is needed to coordinate a building program except in the largest schools. Furthermore, teachers who have training in computers as well as a broad perspective of curriculum are in short supply.

The school library media specialist is ideally suited to coordinate the school's computing program. This person has a background in the selection and management of instructional resources and equipment and an interdisciplinary perspective of the building program. As media professionals move toward the role of information managers, it is natural that they take on the role of "technology coordinators" for the schools.

The building-level computer coordinator should be included in the development of the district plan for microcomputers. This person should also be provided with quality inservice opportunities designed to develop computer competencies. He or she must be knowledgeable about the wide range of ways computers can be used in schools. Especially important is training in the evaluation of computer software and the most effective ways of using computers for teaching.

The principal must also play an active role in the development of the building program. He or she should designate a computer coordinator for the school and support that person in planning and decision making. The principal should include computers in his or her instructional goals and encourage teachers to use computers appropriately in their teaching. The principal's support should include arranging for teachers to attend appropriate inservice and providing time to write curriculum for computer-assisted teaching activities. As the building's instructional leader, the principal must assume responsibility for the building computer plan, monitoring its implementation and clearly communicating the goals of the plan to all staff.

THE BUILDING PLAN

Philosophy and Applications

We have advocated a philosophy of using the computer as a tool to be integrated into curriculum in ways that improve instruction or that allow us to teach something important that we could not teach before. As a by-product of such integration, students become competent computer users without the need for special classes on computing. This overall philosophy must be implemented consistently with the educational philosophy operating in a given building. For example, many junior high schools have an exploratory philosophy of exposing students to many different subjects; as a result of this exploration, they can make choices for high school classes that are experience-based. Providing a variety of introductory computer experiences during junior high, such as computer-generated music and computer-aided drafting, would be consistent with such a philosophy. In high school, where greater specialization is an overall philosophy, students in the vocational program, for example, may learn real-life computer applications which they will encounter in the business world. Learning to use a spreadsheet in an accounting class would be an application consistent with this philosophy.

Applications at the building level will also be influenced by the district-level plan. If, for example, the district plan calls for word processing instruction to take place in the middle school, this application will require a heavy commitment of a building's resources. Having instruction in word processing is not enough; opportunities for frequent practice of this new skill must occur. Such an application might also be consistent with a building goal of improving writing across the curriculum; once trained in word processing, students might be required to use word processing for writing assignments in all classes. Given limited resources, and the understanding that computers cannot do everything in every instructional setting, building leaders must look carefully at the school's philosophy to determine how computing can best be used to improve instruction and learning. Since change is usually accomplished in small increments, a building plan might be implemented in phases, concentrating on one subject area or grade level per year. Integrating computers with instruction must be viewed as a long-term effort that will require ongoing monitoring and evaluation.

Hardware and Software

Decisions regarding hardware purchase are most frequently made at the district level. Building input into equipment selection is essential so that district-level decision makers are fully aware of building goals and needs. Teaching students to use databases might require additional disk drives and upgraded computer memory. An emphasis on word processing requires a larger number of printers. Using computers for classroom demonstration necessitates a large-screen display device. Modems need to be provided for telecommunications applications. District planners must be kept informed of such building needs.

Building-level staff must also be aware of district concerns regarding equipment. If the district has made a commitment to Apple computers, for example, a building must not purchase another brand without consulting with district personnel and considering the consequences in terms of software, repair needs, and the training required for staff and students to use a different system.

Thoughtful selection of software is a critical element of instructional computing. Decisions must be made with close attention to established standards and to building program. The appropriateness of the computer to the content being taught is a critical consideration. Using a software package to test students on retention of the details of a book they have read may not be consistent with the goals of a literature unit. Since existing copyright rules generally require the purchase of one disk for each machine a program is to be used in, wise expenditure of limited budget dollars necessitates that software selection be taken very seriously. Depth instead of breadth must be the rule; it is better to have multiple copies or "lab packs" of a few pieces of well-chosen software than to have single copies of many programs of questionable value. Chapter 4 of this book will describe the selection process in detail.

Inservice

Appropriate inservice is essential to the success of the building program. While the building computer coordinator or media specialist might be expected to provide inservice in some areas, district leadership in this area is critical in order to match training with specific instructional needs. Building inservice needs must be communicated to district leaders, and the two levels must work together to provide inservice that teachers will perceive as being directly relevant to their classroom responsibilities. Chapter 5 describes planning for effective inservice training.

THE COMPUTER LAB

The building plan will include decisions about where computers are to be housed within the school. Research suggests that a "critical mass" of enough machines to accommodate an entire class be kept in one place; in other words, that a computer lab be established *(School Tech News* 1987). Such a lab must contain a minimum of 15 computers, and would ideally house 24 to 30 computers, or enough to accommodate a class of students, 1 per machine. One method for determining the number of machines to be housed in a lab is based upon the number of students in a building, the type of instruction that is to occur, and the estimated length of time required to master the content (Griffiths and Hetrick 1986). Massing computers, rather than assigning one or two machines to each classroom, makes them accessible to everyone in the building and provides the flexibility to use computers in a variety of ways.

Planning for computer labs must be done thoughtfully. The location of the lab is an important consideration. The lab must be in a separate room or area, not a part of a teacher's classroom where its use would be limited to those times when the room was free. It must be housed in an area that is seen as "neutral ground" so that teachers and students do not perceive computers as the domain of a specific department. A location adjacent to the library media center is ideal, since this area is perceived as one which serves all aspects of the building program and is the logical location for the building's software collection.

The layout of a computer lab is often dependent upon the nature of the room or area designated to fill this role and, except in new construction, is often a compromise between the ideal and the possible. Generally, labs seem to fall into two configurations, with computers arranged either around the periphery of a room or in more typical classroom fashion in rows facing the front of the room. Arranging computers around the walls of the room provides for better traffic flow. Teachers can circulate easily around the room to monitor student progress and provide feedback to the students on their work (see Figure 3.1). Anyone who has taught word processing or LOGO

FIGURE 3.1. A "Peripheral" Classroom Arrangement for the Computer Lab

can attest to the importance of this type of "coaching." The peripheral configuration allows for wiring to be tucked behind the computers (Moran 1987). Tables can be placed in the central areas so that students can move away from the computer to do proofreading and revision. A major disadvantage of this arrangement is that students must turn around to face the teacher during instruction. Connecting several computers to one printer can also be difficult in this configuration.

Placing computers in more typical classroom fashion in rows facing the front of the room has obvious advantages for instruction, since students will be facing the teacher, overhead screen, and display devices and will have a writing surface in front of them (see Figure 3.2). Traffic flow, wiring, and supervision of student work pose

FIGURE 3.2. A Typical Classroom Arrangement for the Computer Lab

greater problems in the classroom configuration (Moran 1987).

With either lab arrangement it is important that adequate space be provided for each station. About 36 inches—the width of a standard computer cart—provides room for the equipment and workspace for the student. The height of a standard adult typing table is 27 inches. This height will need to be modified according to the age of the students the lab will serve. Having adjustable chairs also allows for variation in the height of students using the lab.

Wiring of the lab must be adequate to allow for expansion. One circuit per fifteen stations is a standard configuration. A lab must be wired in such a way that the teacher can control computers and monitors from master switches. Certain networking systems allow the instructor to have the output from his or her computer appear on each screen in the lab and to monitor each computer to observe what individual students are doing. Such systems allow software to be stored on a hard disk drive and loaded from that drive into individual computers. Special licensing is needed to use software in this way.

Large-screen display devices for demonstration must also be included in the design of the computer lab. A place must be provided to house the software currently in use in the lab and to store necessary documentation. Bulletin boards enhance a lab by providing a place for informative displays about disk care, lab procedures, and copyright policies. It is recommended that chalkboards not be placed near computers since chalk dust can be harmful to the equipment; rather, erasable boards that can be written on with markers should be provided. If full-time supervision of the lab cannot be provided, windows facing an adjacent classroom or library media center provide for some monitoring of student activities.

The peripheral equipment needed in the computer lab will be determined by the building plan for computer use. If LOGO is to be taught in the lab, adequate memory and color monitors will be required. A word-processing emphasis will necessitate a high ratio of printers to computers; one printer can be accessed by several computers using a switch box (see Figure 3.3). Double disk drives may be required by certain applications such as databases. If telecommunications applications are to be taught, a dedicated phone line must be provided for the lab.

Staffing is a critical consideration in planning a computer lab. Someone must be assigned the duties of scheduling and supervising the lab, providing assistance to staff and students using the lab, keeping track of software, and troubleshooting equipment problems. Depending upon local regulations governing staffing, the lab supervisor might be an hourly employee, who was trained on the job by the building computer coordinator and who is working directly under the coordinator's supervision. The lab supervisor need not have computer experience but must possess a strong interest in learning computing and working with students and teachers. Full-time staffing is essential to the success of the lab for several reasons:

1. Teachers who are inexperienced with computers will feel more comfortable about coming to the lab and bringing their classes.
2. Teachers will be able to send small groups of students from class to work on assignments.
3. There will be someone to assist the teacher during instruction in such areas as word processing, which can be very intensive as each student encounters specific problems that require adult assistance.
4. The security of hardware and software housed in the lab must be ensured.
5. Someone must be responsible for upkeep, troubleshooting, and minor repair of the equipment.

While the central computer lab facility seems to be the best way to provide computers for a majority of applications, flexibility in scheduling equipment must be maintained. Several computers must

FIGURE 3.3. A Multi-Computer Printer Hook-Up

be kept on carts for circulation to classrooms for small-group computer use in simulations or group problem solving. The use of a single computer connected to a large-screen display device as a teacher tool in large-group instruction has also proved to be an extremely effective method of using computers for instruction and provisions for such instruction should be made.

As secondary schools in particular move toward greater specialization in the way they use computer technology, it is likely that buildings may contain several computer labs. These labs will house different types of equipment, depending upon the needs of the program. For example, a business education department may choose to utilize IBM-compatible equipment which is similar to that used in offices. The graphic arts and journalism programs will want equipment that supports desktop publishing. The building plan must take these specialized needs into account.

Computers must also be available to teachers for use as they develop lessons and so that they have the means to become competent computer users themselves. Teachers should have the opportunity to check out computers for overnight, weekend, and vacation-time use. Appropriate insurance must be provided so that teachers are not liable in case of theft or damage to the machines. Cases of good quality must be purchased to protect the equipment whenever it is transported out of the building.

THE "MATCHMAKER"

The need for a building computer coordinator has been described earlier in this chapter. In addition to the planning role, this person must assume the responsibility for overseeing the operation of the computer lab and supervising its staff and for organizing and maintaining the building's software collection. However, the role of this person extends beyond planning for and warehousing computer hardware and software in the building. The success or failure of both district and building plans will ultimately depend upon how successfully a match can be accomplished between the needs of the teacher in achieving an instructional goal and the capabilities of the computer. The building coordinator must be someone who knows the building curriculum, *and* knows computer software in order to make those matches. This "matchmaker" must have knowledge about the planning and delivery of instruction and how it takes place in the various subject areas and must be willing to devote time to finding the "perfect" piece of software to meet instructional needs. This match between software and instruction is a critical piece of a successful program of integrating computers into the curriculum, for unless teachers can see that a new methodology is an improvement over the status quo, there is little motivation to adopt it.

The matchmaker must deal with competing demands for hardware and lab space. With the development of the specialized labs described earlier will come a need for someone to promote interdepartmental sharing of resources. The matchmaker must also be able to recognize the best ways of utilizing computer technology. Clearly, massing computers in a lab setting so that all fifth-grade students can be taught keyboarding is a better use than assigning two computers per classroom to be used as interest centers for students who complete other work. Similarly, learning to organize and manipulate information with a database has greater instructional potential than using computers for drill on math facts, which can be accomplished just as effectively with paper and pencil. The building coordinator must be a person who can make judgments about which uses of computers hold the most promise for improving instruction.

SUMMARY

Careful planning at the building level is essential to the successful integration of computing into the curriculum. A building-level person with knowledge of curriculum, computers, and teaching must be designated to coordinate the school's plan and serve as the "matchmaker" between teachers and software. Creating a centrally located computer lab, which is staffed full-time and contains enough equipment and software to accommodate a class, serves to maximize the instructional use of computers within the general building program.

REFERENCES

Griffiths, John and Deborah Hetrick. "The Facility Concept of the Microcomputer Classroom Laboratory." In *The Microcomputer and the School Library Media Specialist,* ed. E. Blanche Woolls and David V. Loertscher. Chicago: American Library Association, 1986.

Moran, Thomas. "The Ideal Computer Lab from Floor to Ceiling." *Tech Trends* 32 (March 1987): 18–21.

"Study Identifies 10 'Critical Success Factors.'" *School Tech News* 4 (January/February 1987): 1. (Report of study by Terrance Cannings and Jack McManus)

Chapter 4
Software Selection and Management

Selection of software for microcomputers parallels the selection of other nonprint media. In an effort to ensure prudent decisions, selectors of all kinds of software will consider these questions: "Does this software meet a specific curricular need?" "Is it technically sound?" "Is the instructional design effective?" Figure 4.1 illustrates the amount of software one can expect to meet all of these criteria.

FIGURE 4.1. Software Selection Criteria

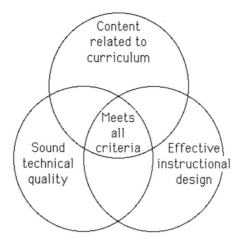

Microcomputer software is used with hardware that possesses capabilities beyond the mere projection of image or duplication of sound. The microcomputer's capability to process individual responses, manipulate data, and keep sophisticated records facilitates user interaction in a way that no other instructional medium can. Therefore the process for evaluating microcomputer software must be structured, systematic, and thorough to ensure that software is not only appropriate for the curriculum and instructionally sound, but also effective in its use of relevant computer capabilities. The key consideration is appropriateness for the curriculum. Even the best designed software merits rejection if it does not match a district's objectives. "The selection of software for preview (or purchase) without a pedagogic purpose in mind amounts to a kind of window-shopping few school systems have resources to justify" (Schiffman 1986, 9). When a district has moved successfully into planful integration (Phase 3—see Figure 1.1), the purchase of software will be based on instructional goals.

Generally, a team-based approach to evaluation and decision making works best. Advantages to this approach are that it allows for maximizing the use of human resources while minimizing duplication of effort and inappropriate purchases. The varying instructional needs, teaching styles, and building philosophy brought to the evaluation process by each of the evaluators will lead to a much sounder decision than is likely to result from a single evaluation.

Although the procedure developed for evaluation of software will vary from district to district, it should provide for the following critical elements:

- Central coordination
- A team of evaluators
- A standard evaluation instrument
- Inservice
- Formative evaluation

CENTRAL COORDINATION

In the early stages of the computer software industry, publishers' catalogs were a common source for learning what was available. As software publishers continue to become more prolific, educators may find reviewing tools helpful in providing some focus. Although reviews do not eliminate the need for previewing software, they are helpful in determining what to preview. As more professional journals carry software reviews, more educators are reading reviews. This results in more requests to preview specific software titles.

It is at this point that the value of a central coordinator becomes apparent. It is the central coordinator who can establish a mechanism for gathering recommendations from district staff, oversee the ordering of software for preview, maintain records, coordinate the evaluation team, publish lists of recommended software, and facilitate a high degree of accountability in general. A central coordinator is able to capitalize on the strengths of individual evaluators and at the same time achieve a balance in the work load. The greatest advantage of central coordination is that it absorbs the tedium of handling previews without jeopardizing staff ownership of the process.

The responsibility for central coordination should be assigned to an individual who:

- knows the district curricula
- is sensitive to and relates well with staff
- is skilled in selection of instructional materials
- possesses exemplary organizational skills
- has support staff to assist with processing preview requests and record keeping

A district media coordinator is one logical person to assume this responsibility since the tasks are identical to those performed in the acquisition of other instructional materials.

A TEAM OF EVALUATORS

An evaluation team can include teachers, library media specialists, and administrators who are familiar with computer-assisted learning and possess a working knowledge of instructional design. Classroom teachers possess content-area knowledge and know when and where to implement a specific instructional strategy to achieve a specific purpose. It is this expertise that must be sought first in the evaluation of microcomputer software. A library media specialist's experience with the selection of all kinds of materials will be valuable. The perspective of administrators as instructional leaders complements the committee.

A STANDARD EVALUATION INSTRUMENT

Districts of all sizes need to maintain consistency in the evaluation process. A comprehensive set of criteria is the tool that will help ensure both consistency and quality. A district can either adopt or adapt an evaluation form that has already been developed and field-tested. One such form, designed specifically for the evaluation of microcomputer software, was developed as part of the MicroSIFT Project of the Northwest Regional Educational Laboratory and funded by the Office of Educational Research and Improvement, U.S. Department of Education (1986) (see Figure 4.2).

The format of this instrument provides a framework that causes the evaluator to systematically examine software for qualities that might otherwise be overlooked. Districts may wish to enhance this form by adding questions that address some specific concerns of potential users, e.g., "How many minutes are required for average use?" "Is student involvement active or passive?" "Describe the social characteristics of the program (competitive or cooperative). Is that positive or negative?" "Is the program most appropriate for individual, small-group, or large-group use?"

The *Evaluator's Guide for Microcomputer-Based Instructional Packages* (1986), which accompanies the MicroSIFT form, breaks down each of the 21 criteria into very specific characteristics. It is a useful resource for familiarizing oneself with the evaluation form or for inservicing first-time evaluators.

While the criteria checklist of such a form is useful in guiding an evaluator through the examination of a software package, the most informative part of the form is that which requires a summarization of the strengths and weaknesses of the package.

An evaluator should ask these questions when completing the summary.

1. Is the content appropriate for this district? Does it meet a specific curricular need? A district implementing the whole-language approach to reading will not have use for even a well-designed phonics program. Nor will a district that focuses on higher-order thinking skills find value in a literature-based package that checks knowledge and comprehension.

2. Does the software allow you to teach something you could not otherwise teach? Does it allow you to teach it better? An effective math facts drill-and practice-package, for example, may not be as efficient as flash cards when one considers the demand on hardware resources. A package intended to instruct learners about dietary fats may defeat its stated purpose in its use of a competitive "numbers game" format. On the other hand, a package designed to teach inferences that provides instantaneous results of manipulation of factors and feedback on responses may facilitate learning in a way not previously possible using a blackboard or overhead projector.

The bottom line is: Will the software allow you to teach better something you need to teach?

3. What are the potential uses? Can it be easily used? If a program is designed for individual use within a large group, such as a word processor, multiple-loading capabilities are a plus. Reliability is another big factor; teachers and students count on being able to use a package when they need it. Reputable companies provide backup copies at no or low cost, supply the user with revisions and updated information, and accommodate replacement of program diskettes.

There are additional advantages to using a consistent set of criteria. A file of the completed evaluation forms is a valuable source of information when questions arise regarding the status of a particular piece of software. The forms are an effective tool for providing producers with feedback regarding their product. When educators fail to communicate what they feel are needed improvements in terms of

FIGURE 4.2. MicroSIFT Evaluation Form

microSIFT COURSEWARE DESCRIPTION   **NORTHWEST REGIONAL EDUCATIONAL LABORATORY**

Title _____ Version Evaluated _____

Producer _____ Cost _____

Subject/Topics _____

Grade Level(s) (circle)   pre-1   1   2   3   4   5   6   7   8   9   10   11   12   post-secondary

Required Hardware _____

Available for Hard Disk? ☐ Yes ☐ No ☐ Unknown   Licensing Available? ☐ Yes ☐ No ☐ Unknown

Required Software _____

Software protected? ☐ Yes ☐ No   Medium of Transfer: ☐ Tape Cassette   ☐ ROM Cartridge   ☐ 5¼" Flexible Disk ☐ 8" Flexible Disk

Back Up Policy _____
Preview Policy _____
Producer's field test data is available   ☐ On Request   ☐ With Package   ☐ Not Available

INSTRUCTIONAL PURPOSES & TECHNIQUES		DOCUMENTATION AVAILABLE:	
(Please check all applicable):		Circle P-(Program) or S-(Supplementary Material)	
☐ Remediation	☐ Drill and Practice	P S Suggested grade/ability level(s)	P S Teacher's information
☐ Standard Instruction	☐ Tutorial	P S Instructional objectives	P S Resource/reference information
☐ Enrichment	☐ Information Retrieval	P S Prerequisite skills or activities	P S Student's instructions
☐ Assessment	☐ Game	P S Sample program output	P S Student worksheets
☐ Instructional	☐ Simulation	P S Program operating instructions	P S Textbook correlation
Management	☐ Problem Solving	P S Pre-test	P S Follow-up activities
☐ Authoring		P S Post-test	P S Other
☐ Other _____			

OBJECTIVES: ☐ Stated ☐ Inferred

PREREQUISITES: ☐ Stated ☐ Inferred

Describe package **CONTENT AND STRUCTURE**, including record-keeping and reporting functions:

Used by permission of Northwest Regional Educational Laboratory. These forms were developed as part of the Northwest Regional Educational Laboratory and funded by the Office of Educational Research and Improvement, U.S. Department of Education.

FIGURE 4.2. MicroSIFT Evaluation Form (cont.)

Estimate the amount of time a student would need to work with the package in order to achieve the objectives:
(Can be total time, time per day, time range or other indicator.)

Strengths:

Weaknesses:

Other Comments:

Used by permission of Northwest Regional Educational Laboratory. These forms were developed as part of the Northwest Regional Educational Laboratory and funded by the Office of Educational Research and Improvement, U.S. Department of Education.

FIGURE 4.2. MicroSIFT Evaluation Form (cont.)

---

microSIFT COURSEWARE EVALUATION   NORTHWEST REGIONAL
                                                        EDUCATIONAL LABORATORY

Package Title _____ Producer _____
Evaluator's Level and Subject Taught _____
Evaluator Name _____ Organization _____

Date _____ ☐ Check this box if this evaluation is based partly on your observation of student use of this package.

Reviewer Statement of Non-Violation of Copyright
   The producer's copyright was respected during this evaluation, and I did not copy or attempt to copy any portion of this package.

   Signature_____ Date_____

SA-Strongly Agree   A-Agree   D-Disagree   SD-Strongly Disagree   NA-Not Applicable
Please include comments on individual items on the reverse page.

CONTENT CHARACTERISTICS

1. SA A D SD NA   The content is accurate. (p. 16)

2. SA A D SD NA   The content has educational value. (p. 16)

3. SA A D SD NA   The content is free of race, ethnic, sex and other stereotypes. (p. 16)

INSTRUCTIONAL CHARACTERISTICS

4. SA A D SD NA   The purpose of the package is well defined. (p. 17)

5. SA A D SD NA   The package achieves its defined purpose. (p. 17)

6. SA A D SD NA   Presentation of content is clear and logical. (p. 17)

7. SA A D SD NA   The level of difficulty is appropriate for the target audience. (p. 18)

8. SA A D SD NA   Graphics/color/sound are used for appropriate instructional reasons. (p. 18)

QUALITY

Write a number from 1 (low) to 5 (high) which represents your judgment of the quality of the package in each division:

_____ Content Characteristics

_____ Instructional Characteristics

_____ Technical Characteristics

---

9. SA A D SD NA   Use of the package is motivational. (p. 19)

10. SA A D SD NA   The package effectively stimulates student creativity. (p. 19)

11. SA A D SD NA   Feedback on student responses is effectively employed. (p. 20)

12. SA A D SD NA   The learner controls the rate and sequence of presentation and review. (p. 20)

13. SA A D SD NA   Instruction is integrated with previous student experience. (p. 29)

14. SA A D SD NA   Learning can be generalized to an appropriate range of situations. (p. 29)

TECHNICAL CHARACTERISTICS

15. SA A D SD NA   The user support materials are comprehensive. (p. 30)

16. SA A D SD NA   The user support materials are effective. (p. 31)

17. SA A D SD NA   Information displays are effective. (p. 31)

18. SA A D SD NA   Intended users can easily and independently operate the program. (p. 32)

19. SA A D SD NA   Teachers can easily employ the package. (p. 34)

20. SA A D SD NA   The program appropriately uses relevant computer capabilities. (p. 34)

21. SA A D SD NA   The program is reliable in normal use. (p. 35)

RECOMMENDATIONS

☐ I highly recommend this package.

☐ I would use or recommend use of this package with little or no change. (Note suggestions for effective use below.)

☐ I would use or recommend use of this package only if certain changes were made. (Note changes under Weaknesses or Other Comments.)

☐ I would not use or recommend this package. (Note reasons under Weaknesses.)

Describe the potential use of the package in classroom settings:

Used by permission of Northwest Regional Educational Laboratory. These forms were developed as part of the Northwest Regional Educational Laboratory and funded by the Office of Educational Research and Improvement, U.S. Department of Education.

programming, packaging, and documentation, producers are put in the unenviable position of "second-guessing" the end user.

INSERVICE

Because the technical qualities of microcomputer software may not be as familiar as those of other instructional formats, there is justification for providing inservice training for those individuals who have been identified to serve on the evaluation team. This inservice needs to include:

- Modeling of both good and bad software.
- Labeling of the qualities that cause the software to be either good or bad.
- Guided practice in using the designated evaluation form.
- Emphasis on these questions: "Does the software meet a specific curricular need?" "Will the software enable us to teach this content better?" "Will the software enable us to teach something we could not teach before?"

Chapter 5 describes the characteristics and qualities to be sought in identifying effective inservice trainers.

FORMATIVE EVALUATION

Formative evaluation is critical to the success of any ongoing process. The software industry continues to change and grow rapidly. Not only is there far more software available than there was five years ago, but there has also been a significant improvement in quality of some types of software. Districts are able to maintain high standards and be more selective. All collections of instructional materials require systematic review and weeding. Removing obsolete or inadequate microcomputer software from a collection should create no sense of guilt or remorse. The process for "deselecting" will depend upon the process used in making the selection in the first place. The critical questions to ask in reevaluating software are: "Has it been replaced by something better?" "Has the curriculum changed so the software no longer fits?" "Is the software less effective than was anticipated?"

THE PROCESS IN PRACTICE

A district's plan for software selection will be determined by that district's organizational structure. The decision-making structure and the degree of formality will affect the personality of the process. How the plan looks is not as critical as that there be a plan. The amount of software sitting on shelves or being used for recreation rather than instruction in many districts is evidence that there is a need for a software selection process.

One process that has worked looks like this:

The district coordinator supplies each building level media specialist with preview request forms. Teachers in each building submit each preview request to their media specialist, who, in turn, forwards it to the district coordinator. The district coordinator verifies the status of the title. If it has already been previewed and approved, the building-level media specialist is notified that it is approved for purchase. If it has been previewed and rejected, copies of the completed evaluation forms are sent to the building. If it has not been evaluated, it is ordered for preview.

When the preview material arrives, the media coordinator identifies three evaluators to examine the software. Content and level of the software are matched with the content-area expertise and grade-level experience of the evaluators. One of the evaluators will be in the building from which the preview request originated. This is to ensure that the requestor is given the opportunity to examine the software. Each evaluator will use the designated evaluation form to assess the software and make a recommendation. The district coordinator then reviews the three evaluations and, in many cases, will also evaluate the software before making a final decision. If rejected, the software is returned to the producer with a copy of the completed evaluation forms. If approved, the software is purchased for the district media collection and is made available for preview by all buildings. Lists of approved software are disseminated to building administrators, media specialists, and subject-area coordinators on a quarterly basis (see Figure 4.3).

SOFTWARE MANAGEMENT

The result of the district software selection process is a list of software relevant to various curricula at appropriate grade levels. It is from this list that computer software purchases at the building level are made. The building-level library media specialist, who makes selection decisions regarding various types of print and nonprint instructional media, selects for purchase from teacher recommendations those titles that are deemed appropriate to the instructional program within the building. The library media specialist and the teacher must consider the instructional needs of the students, looking at the specific units taught within the building, as well as the teaching

FIGURE 4.3. The Software Selection Process

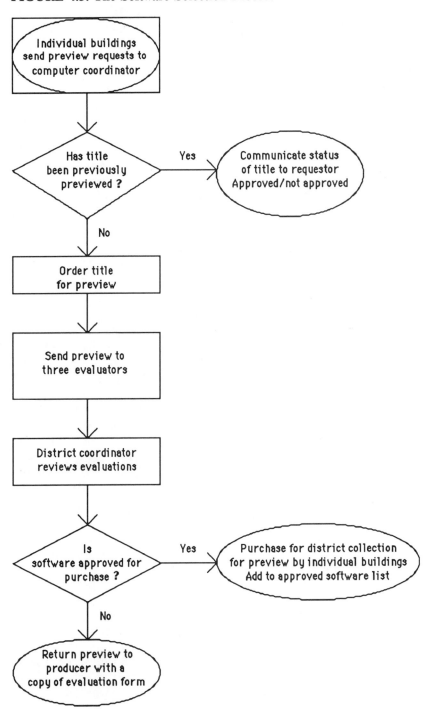

styles of individual instructors. Not every content or skill can best be delivered by a computer program, nor can every teacher comfortably teach with a computer. It is not necessarily prudent, therefore, to purchase everything that appears on a district's recommended list. Rather, purchases should be limited only to that software that enhances the existing curriculum of the building and that will be used by the instructional staff.

One justification for giving the library media specialist the responsibility for coordinating building-level software selection is that he or she knows the range of the curriculum, the specific units, and the teaching styles within the building. The media specialist already has in place a system for meeting with staff to discuss and determine instructional materials needs and for soliciting and acting upon requests for specific materials. Equally important is the fact that in the building's library media program there exists a system for ordering, acquiring, processing, and providing access and accountability for various instructional materials. It is most logical that a sound system for handling other formats of media—from books to magazines to videocassettes to compact discs—could also quite naturally handle the format of instructional microcomputer software.

By integrating software into the library media center's processing system and collection, many potential problems can be averted. Once a decision has been made to purchase a particular program, the library media specialist will, before ordering, determine if the software has already been purchased or if it has been ordered. If the ordering is done by several individuals in a building, the likelihood of duplicating purchases increases.

Once the software arrives, it should be processed for the library media center collection just as any other instructional material is: The software is cataloged (i.e., bibliographic and descriptive cataloging) and classified (i.e., Dewey Decimal system) consistent with the rest of the print and nonprint collection. The fundamental rationale behind this careful processing is increased access and accountability.

ACCESS

All of the instructors likely to use or be interested in a particular software program should be notified immediately upon its arrival in the building. If an individual teacher in the building has ordered a program, he or she may not assume the responsibility of informing other teachers of its arrival. The library media specialist, serving the entire school, has a formal system in place for announcing to the staff all new acquisitions.

Beyond this initial notification, continued subject access to the software is vital to its usefulness. By cataloging the software and filing its card set in the card catalog, controlled access to the software consistent with other instructional materials is provided. When a computer software collection is small, it may be possible for the teachers and the library media specialist to remember and recall each program. As the collection grows, however, it becomes increasingly more likely that a piece of software will be forgotten, buried away on some shelf. Card catalog access ensures that if there is a need for instructional materials on a given topic within the curriculum, any appropriate computer software package will be pulled up along with any other media (books, kits, videotapes) relevant to the topic. This subject access to the software has much greater value than a simple list of the software by title. Many times titles of software packages are either deceptive (Is Power Drill about industrial arts, dentistry, or mathematics?), meaningless (Gertrude's Secrets), or vague (Social Studies Volume 2). By cataloging the packages and assigning the appropriate subject descriptors, the software within a building's collection is found when needed.

Processing computer software to provide card catalog access also serves to integrate this new medium into the mainstream of instructional materials, demystifying it somewhat. "Oh, good! Our collection has seven books, one computer software package, one videotape, and two sound-filmstrip kits on heredity and genetics."

ACCOUNTABILITY

The primary rationale, then, for centralizing the acquisition and processing of software is increased access. The other justification is accountability in terms of money spent, inventory control, and copyright compliance. First, with the library media specialist responsible for coordinating the selection, the building's budget allocation for software will more likely be handled with balance among all areas of the curriculum. Careful purchasing, staff notification of acquisitions, and continual access helps ensure that expenditures in the area of instructional software are judicious and worthy.

Inventory control, including storage and circulation, is another process already in place in the library media center for handling various instructional materials. A centralized collection of instructional materials offers a greater accessibility to a range of users than does a dispersed collection. The same holds true for instructional software. The software is housed where it can be monitored by media staff in terms of appropriate storage, proper organization, and circulation. The software can circulate on the short term (one class period) or long term (the school year), but regardless of how long the software is checked out, accurate circulation records are maintained so that every software package can be accounted for at any given time. If the computer lab is located in the media center, the collection would be housed there. If the computer lab is not within the media center, it would be more logical for the software to be housed as a satellite collection in the lab. In that event, it then would be necessary for the computer lab staff to maintain the circulation and monitor the storage and organization of the software. A thorough inventory once or twice a year will allow the media specialist to determine if the software is still functioning properly, whether it has been lost and needs to be replaced, and how much each program is being used.

A building circulation policy for computer software must be established. The policy should specify whether students can check out software for out-of-building use and whether teachers can restrict the use of specific programs from students. Specific software may be restricted from certain levels of students so that the programs are reserved for use by those in a more appropriate age group or curricular area. Some simulations and problem-solving software programs can be "spoiled" for formal instructional uses if students are allowed to "play" them without proper direction or guidance. The policy should also specify who is responsible for damaged or destroyed software. In addition, the policy should stress the importance of copyright compliance, forbidding illegal copying of disks. A building-level circulation policy is shown in Figure 4.4.

The issue of copyright compliance regarding computer software must be addressed at the district level, with building-level administrators and media specialists responsible for establishing practices to enforce the policy. It is not acceptable for educators to make copies of software for personal or class use, claiming budgetary constraints as justification. We have a legal and ethical obligation to abide by the copyright laws and regulations and to model this appropriate behavior for our students.

The Software Copyright Committee of the International Council for Computers in Education (ICCE) has focused on several issues relating to educational computing copyright. In 1983 the group issued guidelines and a policy statement urging vendors to provide reasonable pricing arrangements for software backup copies, multiple-copy "lab packs," and networking versions of programs, while firmly advocating to consumers the importance of compliance to the 1978 Copyright Act and its computer amendment. The group also recommended that school districts develop, adopt, and enforce a software copyright policy. The ICCE offered a "Model District Policy on Software Copyright" to assist districts in developing an inclusive policy. In 1987 the ICCE reviewed and revised the guidelines to address the changes that have evolved in both education and the marketplace (see Figure 4.5).

The building administrator, the instructional leader of the building, must communicate the district's policy on copyright compliance—the dos and don'ts, the implications for violators—to the fac-

FIGURE 4.4. Building Microcomputer Software Circulation Policy

1) The computer software is housed in the computer lab and is maintained, inventoried, and circulated by the media staff.

2) Staff members may check out software on a long term basis, with software subject to recall if requested by another staff member.

3) Students may check out software for use during a class period in the computer lab.

4) Students may check out software for use outside the school with special permission.

5) Teachers may request that certain software programs be restricted from use by students working independently.

6) Students and teachers must report disk errors or suspected disk damage. If it is determined that intentional damage was inflicted, the individual involved is responsible for paying for the replacement disk.

7) Copyright adherence is mandatory. Neither teachers nor students will be allowed to "copy" each other's or the school's disks.

8) Backup disks are not circulated; they are used only when the original is damaged and is being replaced.

9) One disk will not be booted into multiple computers, unless explicit permission is granted by the software producer.

ulty and staff of the building. Signs can be posted near the computers just as copyright warning signs are posted near photocopiers. A presentation and discussion at a faculty meeting should clarify the issue.

The students must also learn about computer copyright laws and regulations. Ethics in technology is an appropriate topic in the social studies curriculum. But the students will learn more from what they witness. If they see teachers making or using illegal copies, using a multiple-boot process when it is not acceptable, even using the legal backup disk along with the original when the backup is intended for

FIGURE 4.5. **Model District Policy on Software Copyright (ICCE, 1987)**

It is the intent of [district] to adhere to the provisions of copyright laws in the area of microcomputer software. It is also the intent of the district to comply with the license agreements and/or policy statements contained in the software packages used in the district. In circumstances where the interpretation of the copyright law is ambiguous, the district shall look to the applicable license agreement to determine appropriate use of the software [or the district will abide by the approved Software Use Guidelines].

We recognize that computer software piracy is a major problem for the industry and that violations of copyright laws contribute to higher costs and greater efforts to prevent copying and/or lessen incentives for the development of effective educational uses of microcomputers. Therefore, in an effort to discourage violation of copyright laws and to prevent such illegal activities:

1. The ethical and practical implications of software piracy will be taught to educators and school children in all schools in the district (e.g., covered in fifth grade social studies classes).

2. District employees will be informed that they are expected to adhere to section 117 of the 1976 Copyright Act as amended in 1980, governing the use of software (e.g.,each building principal will devote one meeting to the subject each year.)

3. When permission is obtained from the copyright holder to use software on a disk-sharing system, efforts will be made to secure this software from copying.

4. Under no circumstances shall illegal copies of copyrighted software be made or used on school equipment.

5. [Name or job title] of this school district is designated as the only individual who may sign license agreements for software for schools in the district. Each school using licensed software should have a signed copy of the software agreement.

6. The principal at each school site is responsible for establishing practices which will enforce this district copyright policy at the school level.

Used by permission of the ICCE Committee on Software Copyright.

archival purposes only, the students are being sent the message that "softlifting" or "software piracy" is acceptable as long as one doesn't get caught. Students must learn from their teachers' examples that copyright compliance is vital and that the implications for violation are significant.

SUMMARY

A formal approach to evaluation and selection of microcomputer software facilitates a high degree of accountability and accessibility at both the district and the building level. Consistent procedures lead to sound purchases that match instructional philosophies and increase the effectiveness of instruction. Management is critical in the access and use of software. Cataloging helps communicate what is available and provides a mechanism for inventorying holdings. Policies on circulation and copyright delineate expectations of users. The time and energy invested in decision making before actual classroom computer use generates rewarding dividends—successful learning experiences.

REFERENCES

International Council for Computers in Education Software Copyright Committee. "1987 Statement on Software Copyright: An ICCE Policy Statement." *The Computing Teacher* 14 (March 1987): 52–53.

MicroSIFT Project of the Northwest Regional Educational Laboratory's Technology Program. *Evaluator's Guide for Microcomputer-Based Instructional Packages.* Eugene, OR: International Council for Computers in Education, 1986.

Schiffman, Shirl S. "Software Infusion: Using Computers to Enhance Instruction. Part Two: What Kind of Training Does Software Infusion Require?" *Educational Technology* 26 (February 1986): 9–15.

Chapter 5
Teacher Inservice

Training teachers to use computers in their classrooms is a difficult problem for schools. Challenging questions confront educational leaders: "What content should we teach teachers?" "Who can do the teaching?" "Should all teachers be expected to learn?" "Should the content be the same for all teachers?" "When should the learning occur?" "Who has the responsibility—the school or the teacher or the college of education?" While definitive answers to all of these questions may not yet have been found, some of these issues can be addressed.

Early in the 1980s there was considerable pressure from computer advocate groups that computer literacy should be required of all teachers; recommended content included writing a simple program, knowing computer terminology, discussing the history of computers, and discussing the moral and human impact issues related to computers (Martin and Heller 1982). Many teachers who participated in such literacy courses would state that they went on to use very little, if any, of the outcomes of those courses. The content of the courses had little relevance for their teaching. In many instances, teachers took courses but then had little or no access to hardware or software in their classrooms. In short, these early inservice attempts were simplistically planned, isolated events. Instead, inservice must be a part of the general plan. Content, methods, schedules, expectations, and personnel for inservice must be planned in concert with other instructional computing decisions.

Teacher inservice related to instructional computing has as its goal a change in teacher behavior. In order to implement change, instructional leaders must take into account the change process. In *Taking Charge of Change* (1987), several recommendations are advanced for interventions to facilitate change. The change process is described as having six stages of concern. If each of those stages of concern is addressed, change is more likely to be achieved. This has particular relevance when dealing with technology, where high levels of teacher anxiety are common. Stage 0 is characterized as "Awareness Concerns." Inservice leaders can alleviate these concerns by giving teachers enough information about the technology and its usefulness to arouse interest, but not so much as to overwhelm. Further, the more teachers are involved in decisions and discussions about implementation of change, the more likely is success. Stage 1 is characterized as "Informational Concerns." One particularly useful strategy here is to provide clear information about the use of the computer in as many ways as is feasible; examples include communicating in both large and small groups, and providing opportunities to see the intended computer applications in progress in classrooms or on videotape. Stage 2 is characterized as "Personal Concerns." These concerns involve anxiety and require support and encouragement; breaking the change down into small, attainable steps can often help overcome anxiety. In Stage 3, "Management Concerns" arise. For change to occur, all logistical details of hardware, software, and scheduling must be covered. Stage 4 is characterized as "Consequence Concerns." To resolve these concerns, opportunities to hear testimony of successful converts to the computer application can go far in helping teachers accept the possibility of positive consequences. At Stage 5, "Collaborating Concerns" surface. The best approach is to facilitate collaboration and teamwork among persons interested in sharing. At Stage 6, "Refocusing Concerns" arise. At this stage, teachers are ready to transfer their learned skills to other applications and to expand on the new skills. Encouragement is the best way to facilitate. By considering each of these stages of concern in the change process, the inservice leader can alleviate concern and pave the way for teachers to adopt the computer application being advanced. Without addressing these concerns, resistance is likely.

Staff developers must consciously build into inservice those behaviors that will facilitate adoption of change. Figure 5.1 gives a description of types of activities to facilitate a change from teaching problem solving using chalkboard and paper-and-pencil activities to using the computer.

Research on the topic of teacher inservice offers several important guidelines applicable to the question of computer inservice. Georgea Mohlman Sparks (1983) reviewed the research on staff development and summarized some significant factors. Several of those points need to be addressed in designing instructional computing staff inservice.

The content decision is a critical one. There is not necessarily one set of facts or skills appropriate for all teachers to learn. Instead, how the teacher uses the computer in the classroom must be a guiding factor in what is taught in a staff development program. Teacher time is valuable and limited; there must be a sense that what teachers are learning will have direct use for them. Therefore, teacher inservice must be correlated with the overall district plan for com-

FIGURE 5.1. Facilitating Acceptance of Teaching Problem Solving with a Computer

Stage	Facilitating Behaviors
6-Refocusing Concerns	Identify ways to relate problem-solving software dealing with variables to a science lesson
5-Collaborating Concerns	Bring together teachers who are teaching with problem-solving software so that they can share ideas; a users' group
4-Consequence Concerns	Provide opportunities for newly trained teachers to visit classrooms of veterans to observe benefits of teaching problem solving with a computer
3-Management Concerns	Provide software and equipment
2-Personal Concerns	Break down teacher skills into small chunks: nonevaluative feedback, questioning strategy, record keeping, etc.
1-Informational Concerns	Demonstrate teaching techniques to teachers
0-Awareness Concerns	Involve teachers in discussions about the need for teaching problem solving

puter use. At grade levels where word processing will be taught, teacher inservice topics need to be word processing and the prerequisite computer skills for word processing. Examples of prerequisite skills include initializing disks; handling, storing, and protecting disks; and understanding terms like "file" and "embedded commands." Likewise, at grade levels or in content areas where teachers will be expected to use databases, teacher inservice topics need to be databases and the prerequisite computer skills for database management. Examples of prerequisite skills might be understanding Boolean logic or the terms "search" and "sort." Where teachers are expected to use the computer to teach problem-solving skills, the inservice topics need to be related to problem-solving; topics would include questioning strategies, responding to student answers without judging, and using operational skills in setting up and using the equipment. Each classroom expectation can be matched to a teacher inservice program. This prescriptive approach to teacher inservice is similar to the training model seen in business where employees are trained for specific tasks to suit the organization's needs. Clearly, the school district with limited resources must limit its responsibility for teacher training and match its training program to the needs of the organization. Such a match is beneficial to both the organization and the teachers; the organization limits its commitment to meet its immediate needs; the teachers expend time and energy on activities from which they see immediate benefit.

Sparks discusses at some length the scheduling of staff inservice programs. Research she cites suggests that the "one-shot" presentation is much less likely to result in change. Instead, teachers need to be given the content spaced over time to allow time for assimilation. In asking teachers to assimilate the microcomputer into some aspect of their teaching, there must be time to attain the new content, to compare the new learning with prior knowledge and expertise about one's teaching, to practice new skills, and to organize the logistics of schedules, equipment, and classroom management. One session, regardless of length, cannot provide the opportunity for such a process to occur.

Teaching with a computer is a skill. For teachers to develop skill, there must be opportunities for practice, both guided and independent. The trainer must design into the inservice program simulated teaching situations that provide opportunities for practice of specific techniques; specific, nonthreatening feedback on teacher performance is important at this point. In addition, teachers need opportunities to practice each technique independently. Practice opportunities depend on the scheduling pattern of the inservice segments, so that between segments of input there are times for practice. For example, in teaching a word processing program, a segment of input on editing commands should be followed by opportunities for guided practice under the trainer's direction and subsequent independent practice before a succeeding segment on printing options (see Figure 5.2).

Clear, detailed presentations of information with modeling or demonstrations are necessary. Teachers need to see specifically what will be expected of them; they need to have the parts of the model labeled. Much of teacher behavior is a result of following a model; in training teachers, the student teaching experience is a prime example of teaching teachers how to teach via a model. That model has considerable influence on teaching behavior. The majority of today's practicing teachers have had no model for using a microcomputer as a teaching tool. Modeling behaviors for this kind of teaching are essential. The model may take the form of videotaped teaching segments where the computer is used in a demonstration mode with large groups of students. The model may include printed materials that the teacher would use with students in teaching database lessons or word processing. The model may include schedules or schematics for organizing students to use a computer laboratory. Modeling can take many forms, but it is an essential part of the content to facilitate teachers' acceptance of a new way to teach. Models help to make the new teaching behavior more concrete.

Teacher control in some aspects of the inservice is important in diffusing their sense of powerlessness. In a world where curriculum

FIGURE 5.2. Teacher Inservice on Word Processing

decisions, scheduling decisions, textbook selections, and other decisions are made by others, classroom teachers value the opportunity to make some decisions. Although the inservice may be required (and should be), some opportunities do exist for teachers to participate in the decision-making process within the inservice program. Participating teachers might have input on specific content, software selection, class organization, or scheduling.

Identifying effective trainers for teacher inservice in the area of instructional computing is a challenge. Often, the typical trainer is a secondary mathematics teacher who has a personal interest in computers or has some background in programming. While those may indeed be characteristics of some effective trainers, there are some more critical criteria by which we can measure potential for trainers. Often, there is a tendency to focus first on the technological knowledge of the trainer and secondarily on the teaching skill. That is reverse-priority order. If a person will be teaching teachers how to teach with new technology, clearly one characteristic must be that the trainer has been an exceptionally successful teacher. That success as a teacher should have been exhibited by effective design and delivery of instruction. Another criterion is that the trainer must be nonthreatening, either by personality or by position. For many teachers the technology itself will be threatening; the trainer must be able to alleviate anxiety, not intensify it. Knowledge about the technology and discrimination in the appropriate uses of it are also important characteristics. The realization that the microcomputer is not the panacea for all of education any more than any other technology has been is essential, lest the trainer be perceived as a zealot; the perception should be that the trainer is a part of a problem-solving team, identifying ways this technology can meet specific teaching/learning needs. Consistency in the philosophy of the trainer and the organization's philosophy relative to the appropriate place for this technology is important. Teachers in training need to hear consistent messages from their superiors and the trainer. Technical expertise, while important, must be seen as only one of several criteria to consider and, indeed, not the most important one.

Providing logistical, financial, and psychological support for teachers is an important factor in establishing positive teacher attitudes toward staff development. Time released from classroom responsibilities for inservice symbolizes for teachers that the administration values the inservice topic and recognizes the added expectations the new technology brings. A teacher who commits energy to learning a new technology should be confident that the necessary hardware and software will be provided for implementation. Teachers should be paid to write or revise curriculum to incorporate content made possible by computer technology.

A MODEL

Beverly Showers and others (1987) cite coaching as another component of inservice that can enhance its effectiveness. Her survey of the research suggests that teachers are more likely to keep and use new strategies and concepts if they receive coaching, either expert or peer, while they are trying new ideas in their own classrooms.

Development of inservice models that have characteristics cited in research is no small task. One example of such an inservice program is a program that has been developed and implemented for fifth- and sixth-grade teachers. The teachers will use the computer and selected software to teach problem-solving skills. They will use a large-screen monitor and one computer with their classes in teaching these skills. The inservice program is designed to give them the specific skills they need to be successful. The inservice is required of all teachers at this grade level since the skills are part of the fifth- and sixth-grade curriculum.

Session 1. A videotape of a master teacher using problem-solving software is shown to teachers. Teachers are given directions to observe closely the questioning strategies of the classroom teacher. The presenter and the teachers discuss what they've seen, categorize the types of questions asked by the teacher, and review their sequence. The role of the teacher and the role of the computer are also discussed. Teachers are advised that this model and these questioning strategies will be the content of this inservice series. This inservice occurs during time when the teachers are released from classroom responsibilities.

Session 2. The trainer meets with the teachers to select from a pre-selected list a piece of problem-solving software which the teacher will use. The teacher has the decision-making authority here. The trainer advises, but does not decide. During this session, each teacher discusses with the trainer the content of each software title, the match between that software and the class, and the questioning strategies that may suit the specific piece of software. The decisions made here are the preliminary decisions a teacher makes in choosing instructional materials and beginning to design a lesson.

Session 3. The teacher develops the lesson. This is not really a session per se, as this is the time when the teacher is working alone to get to know the software and to begin to develop a line of questioning that might be used with a class to develop the problem-solving strategies. The teacher then develops a lesson design for teaching with the software. The trainer is available by phone to consult, but generally the teacher is working independently.

Session 4. The teacher and the trainer meet to review the lesson design. The trainer may offer suggestions for changes in questions or sequence as needed. This meeting occurs during the school day when the teacher is released from classroom responsibilities.

Session 5. The teacher teaches the lesson to the class. The trainer observes either the lesson or a videotape of the lesson.

Session 6. The teacher and the trainer review the lesson. The focus is on the questions asked by the teacher and their sequencing. As needed, the process is repeated.

The trainer remains available for consultation as needed, but the teacher begins to develop lessons with progressive independence.

This model incorporates many characteristics of effective inservice:

1. The content is directly related to teacher expectations in the classroom.
2. The teacher has some decision-making power in the process.

3. The sessions are spread over time to allow for assimilation.
4. Modeling of the new expected behavior is a part of the inservice.
5. Opportunities for feedback are provided.
6. Logistical support is given in providing release time for inservice.
7. Coaching is provided in the teacher's classroom setting.

SUMMARY

At the heart of instructional computing is the teacher. Teachers, not computers, teach. It is essential that teachers gain an understanding of the capabilities of this technology in order to be able to identify when and when not to computerize their instruction. Next, teachers require specific inservice directly related to the ways in which they will use this technology in their teaching. This inservice may relate to specific teaching strategies like cooperative learning, questioning strategies, and inductive reasoning, as well as the specific use of the technology itself. These strategies for teaching may be critical to the success of the computer activities. Research related to successful inservice should be considered in the design of instructional computing inservice. Content and teacher attitude are critical considerations in developing inservice programs. In the area of technology, attitude can be particularly crucial where trainers may encounter either anxiety, hostility, or at least negativism. Consideration and thoughtful implementation of the factors found in the research related to effective inservice promise some degree of success in teacher inservice.

REFERENCES

Martin, C. Dianne and Rachelle Heller. "Computer Literacy for Teachers." *Educational Leadership* 40 (October 1982): 46–47.

Showers, Beverly et al. "Synthesis of Research on Staff Development: A Framework for Future Study and a State-of-the-Art Analysis." *Educational Leadership* 41(November 1987): 77–87.

Sparks, Georgea Mohlman. "Synthesis of Research on Staff Development for Effective Teaching." *Educational Leadership* 41 (November 1983): 65–72.

Taking Charge of Change. Alexandria, VA: Association for Supervision and Curriculum Development, 1987.

Part II
Computers in the Curriculum

Chapter 6
Introducing Computers to Elementary School Students

A district will wrestle with several issues in determining appropriate uses of computers at the elementary school level. Among them are: When should computers be introduced? What content should be included? Who should be responsible for the instruction?

Unless a district's enrollment and computer inventory are equal, i.e., one computer per pupil, computer usage will need to be prioritized or limited in some way. This is especially true if providing meaningful, relevant experiences is the goal as opposed to providing exposure to develop an awareness. Is depth or breadth the overall objective? Anytime a decision is made to add a new dimension to an instructional program, it must be accompanied by the question, "What must be eliminated in order to accommodate the new?" In the case of computers, careful consideration must be given to two questions: "Does it enable me to teach something I could not otherwise teach?" "Does it enable me to teach something better?"

One way of limiting usage is to designate content areas in which computer applications will be a priority, e.g., math and/or science. Another way of limiting is to decide which applications will be a priority, e.g., word processing and/or problem solving. Specifying the grade levels at which computers will be used is still another way of limiting computer usage, e.g., grades 4 through 12. Depending on the hardware resources available and the degree of learning desired, a district may combine two or more methods of limiting. While the secondary level focuses on word processing, the intermediate and upper elementary level could focus on the use of a computer to teach problem solving. Decisions to limit by content area or application will be driven by the district's instructional program. If the computer meets a specific need in a specific content area, then that is where and how it ought to be used.

WHEN SHOULD COMPUTERS BE INTRODUCED?

One way of limiting at the elementary level is to limit by content area, e.g., math. When limiting computer use to the area of math, there is another factor to be considered—Is the child developmentally ready to deal with the abstractness of the computer? A sound basis for identifying an appropriate level for beginning computer use is found in the philosophies of David Elkind and Ed Labinowicz. Labinowicz (1980) brought interpretation and meaningful application to the research of Jean Piaget.

Piaget categorized the levels of children's thinking into four major stages (see Figure 6.1).

FIGURE 6.1. Piaget's Stages/Levels of Children's Thinking

	STAGE	AGE RANGE *	CHARACTERISTICS
Preparatory, prelogical stages	Sensorimotor	Birth – 2 years	Coordination of physical actions; prerepresentational + preverbal.
	Preoperational	2 – 7 years	Ability to represent action through thought + language; prelogical.
Advanced, logical thinking stages	Concrete operational	7 – 11 years	Logical thinking, but limited to physical reality.
	Formal operational	11 – 15 years	Logical thinking, abstract and unlimited.

*Age ranges quoted represent averages reported for Swiss children. Departures from these ages can be expected for individuals and for different cultures.

Reprinted with permission from *The Piaget Primer: Thinking Learning Teaching*, by Ed Labinowicz. Used by permission of the author and Addison-Wesley Publishing Company. Copyright© 1980.

According to Piaget's categorization, children in kindergarten through second grade, although capable of mentally representing prior experiences to themselves and attempting to represent them to others through language, are unable to apply logic. During this stage, extended periods of play are important. In the formal educational setting during this stage, experiences will focus on concrete three-dimensional objects which children manipulate to visualize and understand basic concepts.

> "The learning of young children is MANIPULATIVE and FUN-DAMENTAL, as opposed to the learning of older children and adults, which is primarily SYMBOLIC and DERIVED. Young children learn through direct interaction with persons, places, and things. They must learn firsthand about hot and cold, sweet and sour, green and red, square and round, up and down, and much

more. This is manipulative fundamental learning for which there really is no substitute" (Elkind 1988, 25).

"Rather than accelerate blindly to advanced stages, Piaget intends that teachers provide children with the opportunities to explore to its fullest the range of thought at a given stage and to build the strongest possible foundation for succeeding stages" (Labinowicz 1980, 158).

Should a kindergarten or primary teacher decide to use software designed to aid in classification by attribute, such as Gertrude's Secrets, that teacher will need to build concrete experiences into the instruction before using the computer. These concrete experiences will include abundant opportunities for the children to get down on the floor and classify objects (attribute pieces) according to attribute (size, color, shape) and then verbalize the reasons behind their decisions to classify as they did. By providing concrete experiences before exposure to the representations of a computer program, the teacher is not accelerating blindly to an advanced stage.

Although the rate at which children pass through these stages varies, most children in the intermediate grades are nearing the end of the concrete operational stage and making the transition into the formal operational stage. In this stage they are developmentally ready to begin to deal with the abstractness of the computer. But even then, a structured introduction to the computer is necessary to help facilitate the transition from a world of the concrete toward the abstract.

Whatever criteria are used for limiting use, one needs to keep in mind that there are acceptable ways to limit computer use. The most important question to answer in determining either the level or the content area is this: "Is the computer the best way to teach this content at this age level?"

WHAT CONTENT SHOULD BE INCLUDED?

A strong posture has been taken on integrating computer instruction into the existing curriculum; however, the need for some prerequisite learning must be acknowledged. What critical information do children need to use a computer? They need to have a working vocabulary of the basic computer hardware and software components. In addition, they need to know how to care for hardware and software, how to load and operate a program, and what their responsibilities are in terms of copyright law compliance.

Just as children can flip a switch and enjoy light or use a phone to talk to their grandmother without knowing the roles played by Thomas Edison or Alexander Graham Bell, so can they effectively use a computer without knowing about the accomplishments of Charles Babbage, Herman Hollerith, or Blaise Pascal. By the same token, a child can operate a whole realm of software without any programming expertise.

At the elementary level it is important that the computer be viewed as a tool for instruction rather than a subject of instruction. Children should be expected to master only that information which is necessary to use computers effectively.

WHO SHOULD BE RESPONSIBLE FOR THE INSTRUCTION?

If computers are housed in a lab, as recommended in chapter 3, the library media specialist is a logical person to assume responsibility for delivery of introductory lessons. If the classroom teacher who plans on using the computer in instruction feels comfortable with the introductory content, then he or she may wish to teach the lessons. If a building has either a part- or full-time computer coordinator, he or she may assume the responsibility.

Regardless of who is responsible for the instruction, content and timing are critical. The primary concerns are that (1) the introductory lessons be taught just prior to the lessons in which the skills will actually be applied and/or practiced and (2) the content include the information and skills necessary for independent use of computers in subsequent applications.

The lesson plans that follow are examples of how the introductory information might be delivered.

LESSON PLANS FOR INTRODUCTION TO COMPUTERS

Lesson 1

Materials needed:
- One complete computer system (keyboard, monitor, disk drive, printer)
- Overhead projector
- Check-for-understanding sheets—one per child
- Transparency of check-for-understanding sheet

Objective: The learner will identify the components of a computer system.

Lesson input: *Hardware* is the generic term for a computer system. Separate components make up a computer system. The components are connected to function as a single unit. Some children may relate this to the components of a home stereo system with its separate speakers, equalizer, receiver, amplifier, turntable, etc.

The hardware components we will be using most often in school include:

- keyboard
- monitor
- disk drive
- printer

Check for understanding: On the overhead projector write: Disk Drive, Keyboard, Monitor, Printer.

Direct the children to label the components of the computer system. Putting the correct answers on a transparency on the overhead projector will provide students with immediate knowledge of results.

Lesson 2

Materials needed:
- One ruined diskette
- Diskettes in dust jackets—one per child
- Overhead projector
- Transparency of parts of computer diskette
- Transparency with terms for check for understanding

Objective: The learner will identify the parts of a floppy diskette, list four rules for the correct handling of a diskette, and demonstrate how to hold a diskette correctly.

Lesson input: The programs used in a computer are called *software*. The programs are stored on floppy diskettes. Students will be using a diskette each time they use the computer; thus learning the correct terminology and care of diskettes is critical. Using the ruined diskette and the transparency, show students the following parts, describing each and emphasizing the following points:

1. Magnetic disk
   - This is where information is stored. (Information is magnetically arranged similar to arrangement on audio cassette or videocassette.)
   - It is thin and extremely flexible (thus the term "floppy").
   - It is fragile.
2. Protective envelope
   - This is the plastic cover that protects the floppy magnetic disk.
   - It is permanent.
3. Read/write window
   - This is the oval opening at the bottom of the diskette where the magnetic disk is exposed.

- The computer uses this access slot for reading from and writing to the diskette.
4. Label
   - This tells what program is on the diskette.
5. Dust jacket
   - This protects the exposed part of the diskette from dust and other hazards.

Because diskettes are extremely fragile, it is important to know how to take care of them so they will be in good condition when they are needed (see Figure 6.2).

FIGURE 6.2. Displaying a Ruined Disk to Children

Rules for handling diskettes:

1. Hold the diskette between your thumb and forefinger with the read/write window away from you. Your thumb should be on the label.
2. Keep the diskette in its dust jacket when not in use.
3. Keep fingers and other objects or soil away from the read/write window. (Fingerprints, scratches, and dust or other particles will prevent the computer from reading information stored on the disk.)

4. Keep the diskette away from the monitor, top of the disk drive, and other power sources. (These magnetic fields can destroy the information stored on a diskette.)

Check for understanding: Using the transparency showing the five parts of a computer diskette, have the children signal with 1, 2, 3, 4, or 5 fingers to identify the correct part as you read the following statements.

1. The floppy circle on which information is stored. *(magnetic disk)*
2. The soft plastic case that is never removed. *(protective envelope)*
3. The place where the name of the program is printed. *(label)*
4. The opening through which information is read by the computer. *(read/write window)*
5. The paper envelope in which the diskette is stored when not in use. *(dust jacket)*

In pairs, have each student list two rules for handling diskettes and tell why following the rules is important.

Guided practice: Give each student a diskette. (1) Have them remove the diskette from the jacket and reinsert it several times, and (2) have them turn the diskette to the direction appropriate for loading into the disk drive.

Lesson 3

Materials needed:
- One computer system for demonstration purposes
- Laminated paper copies of keyboard—one per student
- Lab of computers—maximum of two children per computer
- One program diskette per computer for guided practice in loading a program

Objective: The learner will demonstrate the operation of loading information from a diskette's memory into the computer's temporary memory and will summarize the responsibilities of using software produced by others (copyright compliance).

Lesson input: Program producers have saved programs on diskettes so they can be used by others. Individuals or schools that purchase programs also assume some responsibility—to use the programs within the limitations established by the producer. If the program is *copyrighted,* that means that the program can be used by the purchaser but that additional copies for other machines should not be made. If additional copies are needed, they must be purchased. Someone has worked very hard to produce a program. That person has rights and is entitled to the benefits of the sale of that program. Some programs have been designed to be used in more than one machine at the same time, while others are for use in only one machine at a time. It is important to know what the limitations are—both at home and in school. Programs can be loaded (or booted) into a computer in one of three ways, depending on the situation and kind of hardware.

Instructions for use of Apple II computers:

1. Inserting the diskette in the disk drive before the computer is turned on will cause the program in the disk drive to be loaded automatically when the computer is turned on.
2. Typing PR#6 tells the computer that you want the program in slot 6 to load. The control card that allows the computer and disk drive to communicate is in slot 6 inside the computer. The sequence to be memorized when using this method is:
   Put in the disk
   Control reset
   PR#6
   Press return
3. Pressing CONTROL, OPEN APPLE, and RESET simultaneously will load the program in the disk drive of an Apple IIe system. Hold down the CONTROL and OPEN APPLE keys and tap the RESET key quickly and lightly.

Since the systems are usually already on when the students arrive in the computer lab, they need to know how to load a program by using method 2 if the lab still has some Apple II or Apple II Plus systems. If the lab has only Apple IIe systems, then method 3 will suffice.

Regardless of the method being taught, modeling the process using a large keyboard chart and a computer with a large screen will help students anticipate what to expect when they are actually at the computers. It is especially critical to demonstrate how to use the left arrow key to move backward to correct mistakes when using the PR#6 method. It is inevitable that someone will end up with PR36 the first time around since the "#" and "3" are on the same key.

In addition to knowing how to load a diskette, students will need to know some general rules for computer use.

1. Touch the metal screws under the front of the keyboard to ground yourself. This helps protect the system from static electricity.
2. Press CONTROL and RESET to stop the disk drive when it is running empty.

3. Remove or insert a diskette only when the "busy light" of the disk drive is *not* on.
4. Use PR#6 or CONTROL, OPEN APPLE, RESET to load diskettes. Turning the computer switch on and off unnecessarily is hard on the computer.

Check for understanding: In pairs, have the students list for one another the rules for using the computer and summarize what the user's responsibilities are when using a program.

Guided practice: Using individual laminated paper keyboards, have the students practice typing the instructions for loading diskettes. Then have students go to the computer either individually or in pairs, depending on the number of computers available, and practice loading programs.

REFERENCES

Elkind, David. "Educating the Very Young: A Call for Clear Thinking." *NEA Today* 6 (January 1988): 22–27.

Labinowicz, Ed. *The Piaget Primer: Thinking Learning Teaching.* Menlo Park, CA: Addison Wesley, 1980.

SOFTWARE REFERENCES

Gertrude's Secrets. The Learning Company, Menlo Park, CA.

Chapter 7
Keyboarding and Word Processing

ELEMENTARY LEVEL

Word processing is generally a student's first opportunity to experience the value of a computer as a personal tool. Early word processing software was designed with the adult user in mind; however, in the last few years a number of user-friendly, menu-driven packages designed specifically for the younger writer have appeared on the market. As a result, an increasing number of elementary children and their teachers are realizing the advantages of using a computer to aid the writing process.

Word processing transforms the computer into a sophisticated typewriter, allowing the user to "type" in information, store the information on a diskette, retrieve it later, make changes, store those changes, and print out a clean hard copy.

Accompanying the increasing use of word processors in elementary schools has been the concern that children do not have the typing skills necessary to use the computer efficiently; typing teachers at the secondary level voice concerns about the bad habits children are developing. Software developers have responded with a variety of typing tutorials for the younger user, and experienced typing teachers have begun to give thought to the validity of moving the keyboarding curriculum to the elementary level.

Keyboarding is the technical side of the writing process—learning the placement of keys on the keyboard. Keyboarding skills can be acquired by using a computer tutorial or by participating in a keyboarding class using either a standard typewriter or computer keyboards. Although keyboarding instruction is not as easily integrated as word processing instruction, it is a prerequisite to using a word processor efficiently. If word processing is to become a part of the writing program, then instructional time and computer equipment must be scheduled for adequate keyboarding practice prior to the word processing experience. In order to experience maximum benefit from the use of a word processor, students need to be able to concentrate on developing ideas and expressing themselves. Searching for keys will severely hamper fluency. A district that places little emphasis on the writing process will probably find little need for either keyboarding or word processing. Teaching keyboarding or word processing simply for the sake of doing what everyone else is doing will result in a waste of instructional time. Meaningful application must be an integral part of the instruction in order to justify the teaching of keyboarding and word processing. A district that is already implementing the whole-language approach will readily realize the merit of incorporating both keyboarding and word processing.

THE WRITING PROCESS—THE AUTHORING CYCLE

The whole-language philosophy integrates the teaching of reading, writing, listening, and speaking. The authoring cycle is an application of this philosophy. The cycle begins with the student's active involvement in a wealth of reading, listening, and writing activities. These activities take place in the classroom, the media center, and the home. Reading and listening enable students to add to their own experiences. These experiences help generate a storehouse of ideas and information to use in their writing. Frequent writing opportunities contribute to the student's *fluency.*

A student shares his or her writing with others by requesting an author's circle. This can be accomplished in one of several ways: by holding a conference with a peer, by holding a conference with a group of peers (writer's circle), or by participating in a small-group conference with the teacher and several peers who also have writing to share. During these conferences the student is provided with feedback in the form of suggestions and praise—nonthreatening, constructive criticism. Students use this feedback to revise their work. During the sharing sessions the students focus on *form.*

Form revisions are followed by a two-step editing process. First, students locate and correct as many of the mechanical errors as they can. Dictionaries, thesauri, usage rules, and lists are used in the self-editing process. The second step is to give the writing to the teacher or a student editor for additional editing. The student's primary concern during the editing cycle is *correctness.*

The culminating activity of the authoring cycle is publishing. Each student is given the opportunity to take the author's chair and read his or her writing to the entire class. The reading is followed by a discussion guided by the question: "What did you like about my story?" The answers to this question are processed by the writer and added to his or her storehouse of experiences, ideas, and information. And so begins the next writing activity (see Figure 7.1).

FIGURE 7.1. The Authoring Cycle

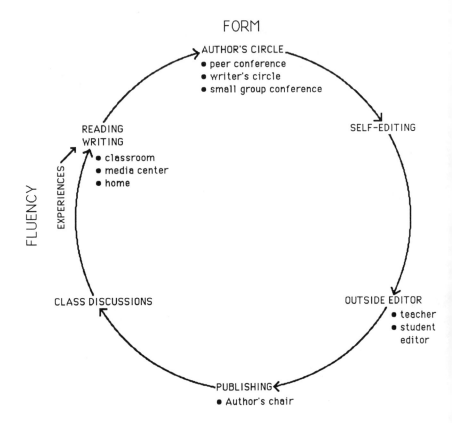

FORM

AUTHOR'S CIRCLE
● peer conference
● writer's circle
● small group conference

SELF-EDITING

READING
WRITING
● classroom
● media center
● home

FLUENCY   EXPERIENCES

CLASS DISCUSSIONS

OUTSIDE EDITOR
● teacher
● student
editor

PUBLISHING
● Author's chair

The implementation of the authoring cycle transforms the class-room into a beehive of activity. At any time during the writing session one is likely to witness a variety of activities occurring simultaneously. Peer conferences occur in several nooks throughout the room. A student with pencil and rough draft in hand is reading to a fellow classmate and is ready to make note of suggestions. At the same time in one corner of the room several students are gathered at a table for a writer's circle, while in another corner of the room the teacher is meeting with a group of students for a small-group conference (see Figure 7.2). The editor's table may be occupied by one or two students who are consulting the tools housed there, dictionaries and thesauri, to assist them with spelling and improving word choice. Others may be visiting the computer lab where they are either composing at the keyboard, making the revisions suggested during one of their conferences, or editing the spelling and punctuation. Still others

FIGURE 7.2. An Author's Circle—A Small-Group Conference

may be at their desks organizing writing folders, recording writing activities for the day, or pondering the next writing project. Because the word processor eliminates the drudgery of recopying with each round of revisions in the authoring cycle, students are able to focus on creating and improving a piece of writing without fear of having to completely rewrite for the sake of producing an attractive final product. This is a critical factor because children become resentful of the drudgery of recopying the work.

KEYBOARDING

Efficient use of a word processor will be realized only if students develop an adequate level of keyboarding skills. Dr. John Stoecker (1987), of the University of Oregon, has conducted research in support of his doctoral dissertation which focuses on the importance of touch-typing instruction prior to the use of a word processor. He determined that the typical student inputs at a rate of 6.5 words per minute, a severe limitation of computer potential. In test-piloting his touch-typing program, he learned that students could increase their input rate to 18 words per minute after 20 minutes of practice per day for 4 weeks. He found 83 percent of the students using correct technique in this research. Recently he determined that the rate could be increased to between 28 and 33 words per minute by providing 25 sessions of 30 minutes in length. The practice of correct technique increased to 90 percent.

In a study conducted in an elementary school in Iowa City, Iowa, during the fall of 1986, 44 fifth- and sixth-grade students were divided into two groups. One group participated in nine sessions of tutorial typing instruction and nine sessions of word processing instruction and practice. The other group participated in 18 sessions of word processing instruction and practice. The pretest and posttest consisted of a five-minute timed typing of the familiar rhyme "Mary Had a Little Lamb." The difference in typing rate increase between the two groups was insignificant. The typing tutorial group increased their rate by 5.39 words per minute, while the word processing group increased their rate by 5.24 words per minute. However, other significant differences were noted. The students who had participated in the typing tutorial instruction could be readily detected in a group of computer operators. They kept both hands at the keyboard with fingers on the home keys, and their body posture was generally correct. Another significant difference was observed in the amount of time required to learn the operation of the word processing software following the typing experience. The word processing program was learned in approximately half the time required by the students who had not had previous keyboarding practice. The keyboarding students were more comfortable with selecting from a menu and far less apprehensive about using the special function keys. The lack of typing rate increase between the two groups may have been affected by a combination of factors.

- Students were divided by reading group to accommodate scheduling; thus abilities were not as heterogeneous as desired.
- There was a two-week break between keyboarding and word processing experience due to the unavailability of hardware.
- The time factor (nine 20-minute sessions) did not allow the keyboarding students to complete all 13 of the lessons necessary to learn the alphabet. On the average, 6.5 lessons were completed.

PREREQUISITES FOR KEYBOARDING AND WORD PROCESSING

Successful keyboarding and word processing experiences can occur only if certain conditions exist. The following are among these conditions.

1. The building or district must have in place a philosophy that focuses on the writing process.
2. There must be enough computers in a lab setting to accommodate at least half of a class. One printer with a switch box connected to a cluster of computers is most effective.

3. The building administration and instructional staff must have a commitment to the writing process and acknowledge keyboarding and word processing as priority uses of the computer hardware.

4. The schedule must be adaptable to accommodate a minimum of twenty 25-minute sessions per student for keyboarding. These sessions must be scheduled on a daily or possibly an every-other-day basis. An erratic schedule or a once-a-week event will not do.

Attempting to accomplish objectives without the above conditions in existence will likely result in an ineffective fragmented approach, a high level of frustration in both teachers and students, and a waste of resources—human, hardware, and time. It would be far wiser to postpone implementation of goals until prerequisite conditions are met. Energies will be better spent on doing something that can be done well with the available resources.

SELECTING A KEYBOARDING PROGRAM

Keyboarding tutorials should be evaluated using the criteria outlined in Chapter 4. In addition, special consideration should be given to the following questions:

1. Does the program model good technique?
2. Is the content correctly sequenced?
3. Is the program easy to implement?
4. Does it include a record-keeping system that provides for self-monitoring?
5. Are lessons designed to be completed within a standard class period? Can the alphabet and most frequently used punctuation keys be learned within the constraints of the building schedule and calendar?
6. Is the cost within the budget? Are lab packs available?

One tutorial designed for the elementary-age keyboard operator that can be easily implemented is MicroType, the Wonderful World of PAWS. The teacher needs no training in teaching typing skills; however, she or he will need to work through the first 13 lessons of the tutorial (alphabet lessons) before using it with children in order to gain some understanding of what children will be encountering.

One whole-group lesson, approximately 25 minutes in length, will need to be scheduled prior to the students' independent use of the tutorial. The purpose of this lesson is threefold: (1) to demonstrate the format of the program and provide practice in getting started, (2) to familiarize students with the record-keeping and management system that will be used, and (3) to enumerate expectations for technique.

Although the program includes a record-keeping system that provides user feedback on typing rate for each lesson, the teacher will want to devise his or her own record-keeping system for two major reasons:

1. All parts of a lesson must be completed within the same class session in order to generate an accurate report. The rate at which students perform will vary significantly within a given class.
2. The record keeping cannot evaluate the observance of correct technique. Speed is secondary to technique; therefore, close supervision and monitoring are critical to reinforce appropriate technique and correct that which is not.

A record-keeping system that works with *PAWS* is one that lists each part of each lesson. Before leaving the computer lab, the student can check off the lesson parts completed, indicating the beginning lesson part for the next session. Most standard grade books lend themselves to this method of record keeping (see Figure 7.3).

FIGURE 7.3. Record Keeping for Keyboarding

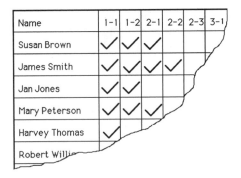

Name	1-1	1-2	2-1	2-2	2-3	3-1
Susan Brown	✓	✓	✓			
James Smith	✓	✓	✓	✓		
Jan Jones	✓	✓				
Mary Peterson	✓	✓	✓			
Harvey Thomas	✓					
Robert Willie						

Another way to teach keyboarding is to employ touch-typing methods, using either a typewriter or a computer keyboard. The teacher responsible for the instruction must be trained in the methods of touch typing. Since few elementary teachers have been trained to teach typing and since the number of available secondary typing teachers may be limited, this method may at first seem unfeasible. Few elementary teachers will be able to take the time to complete the coursework required by higher education institutions. Since 1985, Dr. John Stoecker has responded to concerns of teachers by providing a reasonable alternative—one-day training workshops. The content of these workshops is based on his research and has been field-tested. In these workshops teachers acquire the skill to instruct children grades 3 through 8 in the fundamentals of touch typing. Keyboarding may well be a child's first actual use of computers; it is essential that this initial experience be a positive one. Consequently, districts will want to investigate the pros and cons of both approaches to teaching keyboarding as they determine the instructional program for elementary students.

SELECTING WORD PROCESSING SOFTWARE FOR ELEMENTARY STUDENTS

Chapter 6 discussed the developmental stages of children and the importance of facilitating the transition from the concrete toward the abstract. A word processor appropriate for intermediate-age children will meet the following criteria.

- Simple design. The program need possess only those functions and formatting features necessary for fluency, form, and correctness. Among these features are standard tab indentions for new paragraphs, centering for titles, single and double spacing, movement of blocks of text, and both single-character and block delete. Formatting is not critical when the focus is on the writing process. When formatting becomes a critical issue, as it does in creating student newspapers, the students can adapt to another word processor, knowing that the concepts they have mastered while using one word processor will transfer to another word processor.
- Menu-driven (as opposed to command-driven). Being able to choose from the options on the screen will create far less confusion and error than having to keep track of a list of command codes that carry little meaning for a child.
- Representational icons for basic concepts. The concept of storage and retrieval of intangible documents and information can be overwhelming. Young children need to be able to relate the abstract or intangible concepts to concrete objects with which they are familiar. A graphic on the screen of files in a file drawer with the names of the individual files on tabs will help children visualize what is happening when they use a word processor (see Figure 7.4).
- Multiple-load capabilities. A word processor designed to be loaded into more than one machine is affordable.

One package that meets these criteria is The Milliken Word Processor. It is a reasonably priced, easy-to-use package which meets the needs of the authoring cycle process.

FIGURE 7.4. Concept Figures

Reprinted with permission of Milliken Publishing Company, St. Louis, MO.

Sample lesson plans for introducing The Milliken Word Processor to fourth-grade students follow.

Lesson Plans for The Milliken Word Processor

Lesson 1

Materials needed:
- One complete computer system with large-screen projection device
- Computer lab
- The Milliken Word Processor
- File Cabinet (Data) Diskettes, one per student

Objective: The learner will demonstrate the process of using "writing tools" to enter a short passage, file it, and leave the computer ready for the next user.

Lesson input: (1) Explain and model the multiple-loading capabilities of the word processor, the function of the File Cabinet Diskettes, and the management system for the diskettes. A three-ring binder with plastic sleeves for diskette storage facilitates alphabetical arrangement by student's last name. (2) Demonstrate the wraparound feature since this may differ from the "return" used in a keyboarding tutorial. Review cursor movement, delete, and shift keys.

Guided practice: Students will use their individual File Cabinet Diskettes to enter and save a short common text for editing in the next session, e.g., "Mary Had a Little Lamb." Monitor student performance closely to ensure that everyone follows the steps necessary to save text.

Lesson 2

Materials needed:

- One computer system with large-screen projection device
- Computer lab
- The Milliken Word Processor
- Students' File Cabinet Diskettes

Objective: The learner will demonstrate his or her understanding of temporary and permanent memory by retrieving a copy of a file from the File Cabinet Diskette, making changes, storing those changes, and exiting the word processing program.

Lesson input: Computers have permanent and temporary memory. Permanent memory is the information that is built into a computer when it is manufactured. It is permanent because even when the computer is turned off or unplugged, the information in memory is not lost. Permanent memory contains the information that a computer needs to be able to function and communicate (its language). Its technical name is ROM, which is an acronym for read-only memory. That means that the user cannot change it or write any new information in it. ROM is contained in a chip inside the computer. (Lift the cover and point the chip out.)

A computer's temporary memory is RAM, an acronym for random-access memory. RAM is the place where the computer keeps the copy of the program that we load from the diskette. It is also the place where it keeps information we input through the keyboard or some other input device. It is called temporary memory because it is lost when the computer is turned off. Therefore it is important that we save any important files on our File Cabinet Diskette before we leave the computer. RAM is also in chips inside the computer. (Point out the location. The *Apple Owner's Manual* is helpful in locating RAM and ROM chips.)

When we get a file from the File Cabinet we are actually getting a copy of the file so we can work with it in the computer's memory. The original stays intact on the disk until we put a corrected or changed file in its place.

Modeling: Make changes to "Mary Had a Little Lamb"; e.g., change "Mary" to "William"; insert adjectives to modify "lamb"; change "lamb" to another animal, etc.

Guided practice: Ask students to get from the File Cabinet the copies of the files they saved during the previous lesson. Encourage them to make a variety of changes, e.g., centering the title, etc. Instruct them to save their changed copies in place of the old files so they will be able to print them out during the next lesson.

Lesson 3

Materials needed:

- One computer system with large-screen projection device
- Computer lab with clusters of computers connected to printers via switch boxes

Objective: The learner will print a copy of his or her revised file.

Lesson input: Explain and model the "select"/"online" feature of printers and the switch box controls. Require students to form-feed one extra sheet each time they print to help reduce jamming. Demonstrate choosing the typewriter function and selection of final features. Print edited text.

Guided practice: Direct students to get copies of the files they edited during the previous class period, and have them take turns printing so each student will leave with a hard copy in hand.

Independent practice: Students will use the The Milliken Word Processor for writing, editing, and printing assignments as part of the authoring cycle and/or content area writing assignments.

SECONDARY LEVEL

Word processing at the secondary school level involves a few key changes which must be addressed. First, it is quite likely that a formal, required course in keyboarding and word processing is offered in the secondary school's curriculum, probably within the business department. For years secondary schools have been staffed with trained typing teachers who have taught keyboarding and typing skills first on manual typewriters and more recently on electronic typewriters. The courses were offered within the business education department and generally consisted of a basic typing class which was required of all students, and advanced typing classes for students who planned careers in the business community. Today word processors have essentially supplanted typewriters in the business world as well as in education, and the traditional typing courses are now being revised to accommodate the new technology. The ability to keyboard and word process is no longer considered a business skill, but rather a personal life skill which every student should learn and practice.

The advantage of this situation, where the typing teacher handles the keyboarding/word processing instruction, is that it is administratively easier to schedule all of the students into the course. At a given point in the school year, every teacher in the building can assume that every student has word processing skills and so the teacher can use word processing activities or require word-processed reports from the students.

A limitation of this type of instruction is the danger inherent in teaching a skill isolated from its relevant application. The most relevant application for word processing is in facilitating writing. If the students are only learning the mechanical steps of word processing, the commands and procedures divorced from the context of composing, it will be difficult for them to perceive the value of word processing in the writing and revision process. To guard against this situation, the word processing teacher must work closely with other content-area teachers who require writing of those students to develop meaningful, relevant activities that will teach the students not only word processing mechanics, but also the value of word processing to the writing process.

WRITING—PROCESS AND PRODUCT

At the elementary level, the "authoring cycle" has evolved as a major process for developing the students' writing abilities. At the secondary level, a similar type of writing process is often in place, but another concept has additionally been stressed in many schools: "writing across the curriculum." This philosophy calls for all teachers, regardless of their content area, to become teachers of writing, requiring writing of the students, modeling appropriate writing techniques, providing feedback and evaluating their work, and, above all, demonstrating to students that writing is a vital form of communication, necessary in divergent disciplines.

Teachers of writing concern themselves with both the process and the product of writing. The word processor facilitates both process and product, but its use takes on different emphases depending on the sophistication of the writer. While there is certainly value in using word processing with very young writers, the word processor acts primarily as an output device, a publishing tool. Novice writers value the word processor because it is easier for them to create documents using the computer than it is to handwrite or even type the paper. Young writers are being exposed to the steps involved in the process of writing when using a word processor, but the primary benefit from using a word processor in their writing is a better product. While inexperienced writers do make editing changes in successive drafts of their work, most of the changes are of a more superficial nature: correcting typographical, spelling, punctuation, and grammatical errors, and perhaps even changing a sentence or adding details to the end of the text. But not until their writing skills become more advanced do students begin to revise more extensively, expanding ideas, reorganizing thoughts, looking beyond the surface of the work. It is at this stage that the word processor begins to exhibit its inherent value to the process of writing.

Another change, then, that occurs at the secondary level is that students who have mastered one word processing system, such as Milliken, may now need to be "retooled" on another system. As their writing becomes more sophisticated, the students need a word processor that can perform the editing, formatting, and printing functions they need for making their writing, revising, and finished products match their needs and expectations.

WORD PROCESSING FEATURES FOR SECONDARY STUDENTS

When students reach a more advanced level of writing, it becomes important that they use a word processing system that can perform specialized editing features. The find/replace function allows the writer to locate designated words or phrases used in the document and replace them either globally throughout the document or individually, with consideration of each occurrence. Features such as move, cut and paste, copy, and delete offer the writer the ability to make blocks of text, from words and phrases to paragraphs, dance across the screen electronically, to get at the concept of structure and organization in writing from the small unit of phrase to the larger picture of the entire document.

The ability to perform these editing features in as few keystrokes as possible is another important consideration. The technical features of editing and formatting are accessed through a menu in some word processing programs (such as Appleworks) and through control characters in others (Applewriter or FrEDWriter). A student is less likely to experiment with text manipulation if it is cumbersome to carry out. The length of file allowed by the system is another consideration. An experienced writer could quickly fill up a file in some systems. Related to this is the ease with which the system allows the writer to combine files and move or copy portions of text from one file to another. Again, this is a feature that a more experienced writer will find useful.

Formatting and printing functions also become important considerations with older students. They need to be able to underline, boldface, superscript and subscript, and double- and single-space within the same document to produce the end products desired or required. Control over page breaks, centering, right and left justification of text, and font variations are other useful features. Again, the ability to control these functions easily is important.

Secondary school students should have available to them some of the software designed to facilitate effective revision skills through text analysis. The compatibility of a word processing program to various text analysis programs should be considered when selecting the word processing program. Spelling and grammar checker programs can be used with some word processing programs to highlight problem points in the text for the student to consider and correct. For example, Sensible Speller works with many ProDOS-based programs to read the text of the word-processed document, matching the words against a stored "bank" or dictionary. It identifies words with possible misspellings, showing them in context, enabling the writer to make necessary corrections. Similarly, Sensible Grammar checks word-processed documents for misused phrases and punctuation errors. It should be noted that while these text analysis programs will never replace a teacher in providing comprehensive feedback to a writer, they can assist self-editing of surface writing problems, allowing the student to correct some errors before submitting the document to the teacher.

One word processing program that contains many, but not all, of the features desirable for use by more advanced writers is FrEDWriter, a command-driven, relatively easy-to-use program for the Apple II computer. The chief advantage of FrEDWriter over virtually any other word processing program is its cost. FrEDWriter is free and intended to be copied, enabling the writing teacher to give students their own copies of FrED to use at school and at home. FrED takes its place as a basic school supply along with the notebook, the ruler, and the pencil case!

TEACHING THE WRITING PROCESS

The word processor is not the answer to all writing problems. Simply teaching students how to use the word processor and making the technology available to them will not necessarily make them more creative or proficient in their writing, nor will it automatically make them more critical, conscientious self-editors. Instruction in word processing must not replace instruction in writing. Word processing can facilitate writing—specifically experimentation, revision, and output. But the writing process must be taught through appropriate modeling, carefully crafted and guided writing activities, and constructive feedback (Balajthy, McKeveny and Lacitignola 1986-87).

The word processor itself can be used by the teacher as an interactive tool in several ways to help teach the writing process. One method for incorporating the word processor into the teaching of writing involves using "activity files," which are text files composed by the teacher and saved to multiple copies of the disks. The students load the files, read the instructions written at the start of the file, and then experiment with reorganization of sentences or paragraphs, transitions, description, or whatever writing skill the teacher has in focus for the particular file. Students can save their revisions and submit them for teacher feedback, either on the disk or printed out (Rodriguez 1986).

For example, students could be instructed to load a specific file into the computer from activity disks. The file contains a brief essay or story in which all of the sentences are short and choppy. Students read the essay, and then try to improve the texture of the work by combining sentences or ideas with the use of conjunctions or subordinating phrases or clauses. Students use various editing features of the word processor such as delete, move, or cut and paste, saving their changes of the text on the disk, printing out the newly revised file, and submitting the printout to the teacher for comments. Or, rather than printing the file, the student could submit only the disk containing the file revision which the teacher would later load and read, perhaps "writing" the comments or suggestions in the same file for the student to load and read. Another possibility for feedback is for the teacher to move around the word processing lab, acting as a writing coach, offering suggestions for on-the-spot improvement.

Another lesson making use of activity files teaches students the need for clarity or variety of word choice in their writing. The file the student loads into the word processor contains a passage that uses the same words or phrases repeatedly. The student is instructed to locate the overused words and replace them with others which provide more description or accuracy. This activity gives students dictionary and thesaurus practice. Again, the altered file is saved and submitted to the teacher for feedback.

Some of the commercially developed writing activity files on the market are designed to be used with one word processing program or another. The Bank Street Writer Activity Files encourages writing fluency and revision in its exercises. Some word processors aimed at the education market, such as FrEDWriter, allow the teacher to easily create "prompted" text—on-screen prompts, hints, or instructions—to better guide students through writing activities on the word processor.

A second method for using the word processor to help teach the writing process is to connect a computer to a large monitor or projection device and actually model for the students how to revise a passage of text, pointing out the problem areas and explaining and demonstrating how to improve the writing. For example, the teacher could write a brief essay in which paragraphs and sentences within the paragraphs are out of sequence. Students are given printed copies of this jumbled document to study, and working individually or in pairs, try to devise ways to rearrange the text to improve its structure and logic. The teacher then displays the file using a computer connected to a projection device, and makes corrections to the composition as suggested by the students. Different revisions could be attempted and evaluated by the entire group. Another possibility is to use this technique with a piece of student writing. As with all peer evaluation exercises, the teacher needs to keep the environment nonthreatening. This can be a very effective technique, for students are given the opportunity to see each other's work, praising the positive aspects of the writing and offering constructive comments for improvement in a cooperative "writers' workshop" setting. Also, modeling with actual student writing gives special interest and immediacy to the students: it is quite likely that a problem exhibited in one student's writing is also present in others' writing.

SUMMARY

Word processing is a powerful tool for today's writers, affecting both the writing process and product. It has uses with elementary-age students, complementing the "authoring cycle." Word processing is also valuable to more sophisticated writers as a personal tool, facilitating the writing and revising processes. When word processing skill is taught, consideration must be given to developing keyboarding skills and to providing relevant writing applications. The word processor can also serve as a useful tool in teaching various writing concepts and techniques through activity files and whole-group modeling of the writing/revising process.

REFERENCES

Balajthy, Ernest, Robert McKeveny and Lori Lacitignola. "Microcomputers and the Improvement of Revision Skills." *The Computing Teacher* 14 (December–January 1986–1987): 28–31.

Iowa City Community School District. *Literacy Guide for the Iowa City Community School District.* Iowa City, IA: Iowa City Community School District, 1986.

Rodrigues, Raymond J. "Creating Writing Lessons with a Word Processor." *The Computing Teacher* 13 (February 1986): 41–43.

Stoecker, John, Adjunct Professor, Training and Development. Interview, 23 December 1987, Eugene, OR.

SOFTWARE REFERENCES

Appleworks. Apple Computer, Inc., Cupertino, CA.

Applewriter. Apple Computer, Inc., Cupertino, CA.

Bank Street Writer Activity Files. Scholastic, Inc., Jefferson City, MO.

FrEDWriter. SOFTSWAP, Redwood City, CA.

MicroType, the Wonderful World of PAWS. South-Western Publishing Co., Cincinnati, OH.

The Milliken Word Processor. Milliken Publishing Co., St. Louis, MO.

Sensible Grammar. Sensible Software, Inc., Birmingham. MI.

Sensible Speller. Sensible Software, Inc., Birmingham, MI.

Chapter 8
Teaching with Databases

Just as word processing use grew out from the business community to education, so has grown the use of another computer utility: database management. Database use in education has generally begun with administrative applications. Information for personnel files and student records is entered into a database management system to facilitate the storage and retrieval of that information. The school library media center's circulation files and card catalog are automated by entering bibliographic data into specialized, sophisticated database management systems, enhancing access to materials and streamlining clerical tasks. Classroom teachers are creating computerized grade books by entering student data and grades into database and spreadsheet management programs, again facilitating record keeping, grade analysis, and reporting.

The computerized database, frequently used as a management tool, also has a place in the classroom as an instructional tool. There are three distinct reasons for introducing students to databases and designing instruction which makes use of them. First, by teaching students about databases and the skill of manipulating a database, they are learning a vital "information age" concept and skill. In his landmark book, *Megatrends,* John Naisbitt describes the transformation of our country from one of an industrial society to that of an information society. He quotes figures from a study which found that nearly 90 percent of the new jobs created in the 1970s were related to information, knowledge, or service, while only 5 percent were in manufacturing, long the backbone of our economic system. While some, such as Theodore Roszak, author of *The Cult of Information,* discredit this notion of information as a commodity replacing industry, it is nevertheless true that our students today are entering into a technology-driven, information-rich society where skill at using technology to access information is essential.

Professionals in such diverse fields as medicine, engineering, education, and business tap into online bulletin boards and databases for the most up-to-the-minute notices and information. Travel agents use telecommunication technology to book flights and hotel accommodations, and brokers use telecommunications to buy and sell investments for clients. Secretaries store vast amounts of information and data within sophisticated automated business offices. Store clerks in inventory control and sales carry out their tasks using databases controlled by bar code reader technology. Even in everyday life, computer technology is present to give us information assistance. Grocery stores have terminals—automated "You are here, the oranges are there" databases with graphic maps—to help customers find the desired products. Hotel lobbies have similar terminals to inform visitors of local places of interest and events to help them find resources to fit their needs or interests. Any awareness, insight, or experience our students can gain about databases—the basic unit for most information management in society—will be an edge for them.

A second reason for using the database as an instructional tool is that it provides a means for teaching higher-order thinking skills. In Chapter 10, several specific pieces of software are identified, essentially devoid of content, designed to focus on thinking processes rather than any particular content. Some of the higher-order thinking skills addressed by this software are classifying, comparing, contrasting, drawing inferences, hypothesizing, generalizing, and using Boolean logic. Using a database requires that these same skills be utilized, but this time with some content added. The content of the database can range from vital statistics of animals to demographics of various countries to bibliographic information and reviews of books. Regardless of the content, though, students can be guided to use various higher-order thinking skills. The operational word here is "guided;" the questioning strategy used by the teacher is of critical importance to the development of the thinking processes.

To illustrate the type of questioning strategy a teacher might use, consider an introductory database lesson where the students are working in pairs at computer stations in a lab. They each perform assigned searches of a locally created database which contains information about each of them, first determining the correct search statement or strategy, then performing the search by manipulating the database. A very simple question would ask, "How many students are in Mr. Smith's homeroom?" A follow-up question, "How many students would you predict in Mr. Smith's homeroom were born in August?" requires that students hypothesize and use their experience with Boolean logic to predict a smaller number than found in the earlier question. To perform the search the students must develop a search statement based on the Boolean connector concept (Smith's homeroom AND August). Drawing inferences could be approached by asking students to determine if there is a correlation between the number of books a student reads and the number of hours of television watched. The student would (1) make a hypothesis based on his or her knowledge; (2) develop the appropriate search statement; (3) perform the search; and (4) analyze and evaluate the results, considering outside factors not covered which could affect the results. The importance of structure and appropriate teacher guidance in using databases instructionally must not be slighted. Students usually cannot and will not ask the right questions of themselves. A recent study found that the levels of content learning and skill transfer among students who were guided through structured computer database activities were significantly higher than those of students who were free to manipulate and examine on their own the same data found in a "manual" database (card file). When guided through database use, students develop key information processing skills such as identifying the information relevant to solving the problem, identifying sufficient information for solving the problem, and sorting or arranging the information in ways likely to produce a problem's solution (White 1987).

Beyond serving as a tool for teaching higher order thinking skills, the database can also serve as an instructional vehicle for imparting a specific content. This, then, is the third reason for teaching with a database. In any given curricular area, in any particular content, the classroom teacher is faced with selecting an appropriate method for putting the content across to the students in the way which will most effectively and efficiently bring the students to attainment of the objectives. Perhaps assigning readings or lecturing will get the content across. Perhaps a film or a worksheet or a guest speaker would work. Perhaps a lab experiment or a research activity is the method of choice. Once students understand what a database is, how to develop a search statement, and how to manipulate a database to perform a given search, the classroom teacher could choose the database as the tool for teaching content. By interrogating and manipulating a database, students can gain insight into the subject matter, putting together relationships.

Thus far, only the situation of students using databases has been described. Students are using databases created either commercially or by the teacher to solve problems, classify, draw inferences, or see trends. Skills may be furthered by students building a database. At this stage, students must do research, gather appropriate information, check the information's accuracy, and then enter the information into a database "template"—a blank record with fields established by the teacher. At the next stage the student designs the file, making content, format, and layout decisions, as well as performs the data gathering (Hunter 1985). Higher-order thinking skills required at the database building and design stages include analysis of a problem, categorization and evaluation of information, and conceptualization of a body of information as to its critical attributes, identifying key concepts and eliminating the nonessential (Schiffman 1986). These later stages also lend themselves to cooperative learning/problem-solving activities when groups of students confront an informational need and address how to satisfy it most efficiently and effectively. By building and designing databases, students are learning valuable lessons about information management: that any tool has limitations, that one must be critical of one's own design, and that despite an information glut facing us, data can be organized, controlled, and manipulated to elicit meaning (Thomas 1988).

For students to truly master database management skills, for them to realize the value and appreciate the power that database skills give them, they must be given numerous varied experiences or applications where different types of tasks must be performed or problems solved requiring data manipulation and analysis. "The virtue of database files lies in their logical structure and the fact that they can be used to overlap subject areas in an interdisciplinary fashion" (Hodson 1986, LC 13).

Numerous database packages are being developed and marketed which tie to various content areas. Many of these consist of very simple database programs containing informational files on topics such as states, countries, animals, drugs, careers, and natural resources. The documentation generally includes instructions on how to manipulate that particular database as well as suggested activities and student worksheets.

Other database products consist of the files only and are designed to be used with one of the several standard database management systems such as Bank Street Filer, PFS: File, or Appleworks. These "application packages" designed to accompany leading database management programs are becoming much more common and could perhaps become the most widely used type of computer software in schools.

Several considerations should be made before purchasing either type of database. First, with a product which consists of a simple database management program and file, consider the capabilities of the database program. Some are quite limited in the type of searching allowed. Others do not allow a teacher to add to and/or change the data in the files. The capability to adapt and update files increases its usefulness and relevance. Other evaluative criteria such as multiple copy availability, the appropriateness of the content to the curriculum and the students' level, the accuracy of the information, the ease of use, and the quality of the documentation should be considered. These criteria were discussed fully in Chapter 4.

An alternative to purchasing the commercial database and file package is to develop database files locally for use with a single, database management program such as PFS or Appleworks. There are several advantages to this approach. Students would only have to learn how to manipulate the commands and master the searching procedures of one program rather than having to retool for each new database activity. If they don't have to spend so much time learning the database procedures, more time can be devoted to the content and thinking skills involved in using the database. Also, by creating the database files locally, the teacher can include precisely the content information desired—a perfect match for the curriculum and the level of the students. But researching and generating a database, especially a complex one, and developing the activities and materials to guide the database use can be a very time-consuming task. Publishers will begin to develop more database application packages, perhaps even marketing databases to accompany textbooks in disciplines such as social studies and science, in much the way drill-and-practice or game software has been marketed to accompany some math and foreign language texts. The text would provide the traditional, narrative-type of coverage of a particular topic while the accompanying database file would offer vast amounts of information for students to explore, analyze, and evaluate (Olds 1986).

There are some practical considerations to be made before diving into database use in the classroom. These questions should be asked:

- When should students be taught database skills?
- Who should teach the database skills?
- Which database management system should be used?
- What computer hardware is needed?

WHEN SHOULD STUDENTS BE TAUGHT DATABASE SKILLS?

Although some database programs on the market are designed for use with students in the elementary grades (Beginning Bank Street Filer, MECC's Bookworm), most elementary-age children will not be able to comprehend the logic behind searching a database. While they may understand the essential database concepts such as file, form, and field, and may even learn to perform simple searches, the logic of creating and combining sets (Boolean logic) involves formal operations, which most children are developmentally incapable of until around junior high age. Teaching in-depth database skills to elementary children would be comparable to trying to teach the abstract notion of ratio in math to very young children. Therefore, junior high is an appropriate time for teaching students the core skill of using databases.

WHO SHOULD TEACH DATABASE SKILLS?

There is no one best person to teach database skills to the students. A content-area classroom teacher who is enthusiastic about using a database instructionally is very appropriate. He or she would be motivating and would provide a relevant application for using the skills once the students have mastered them. Skills taught in isolation, without any visible connection to the students' classwork, are not learned enthusiastically or well. For example, teaching students how to use a sewing machine or the card catalog if they have no immediate use for the skill is ineffectual. Therefore, any skill is best taught when integrated into the curriculum.

The library media specialist could also logically teach database skills to the students. The skills could be approached as another set of media skills which, once mastered, will help students locate information. This approach would also facilitate teaching the skills to all of the students. This is helpful if the skills are to be integrated by content-area teachers, who could at some point assume that all of the students have learned to use a database, and would not need to devote class time to teaching skills, but rather focus on content. The library media specialist must coordinate the teaching of the unit with content-area teachers, though, so the skills are not taught in isolation, but as a basis for an upcoming or concurrent classroom application.

Another possibility is to divide the responsibility of teaching the skills. A classroom teacher or the library media specialist could introduce the database concepts and could show how to manipulate the program, and a math teacher could teach the Boolean concepts of sets and connectors (AND, OR, NOT). This type of team teaching requires careful planning and scheduling, but is effective.

WHICH DATABASE MANAGEMENT SYSTEM SHOULD BE USED?

A general rule to follow is to select software before hardware, to let the software dictate, rather than being limited by the inflexibility of the hardware. Most schools, though, already have some hardware, so limitations are already in place before the selection of a database program. (Few schools could afford to throw away a lab of 30 Apple IIe computers and replace them with 30 Macintosh computers!) Important software considerations in addition to standard evaluation criteria such as ease of use, cost, and quality of documentation include:

- Power or capacity. A program which can only hold 50 single page forms might work for simple database files but does not offer enough versatility. After using databases more, one will see other applications which might require greater capacity.

• Speed. A database program which performs searches slowly can be a big time waster in an instructional setting. There is a vast difference in sorting and searching speeds among database management systems.

• Open/locked files. When students search a file, can they also accidentally (or intentionally!) change the data? This can be most inconvenient. Look for a program where the "update" or "add" feature is separate from the "search" feature.

• Printing capabilities. How flexible is the formatting? Is it possible to dump a screen and to sort on numerous fields (first, second, third, etc.) before printing?

• Compatibility with word processing programs. As the students begin to accept the database as a source of information, they may turn to it when doing research on various topics, just as they consult encyclopedias or almanacs. The ability to transfer data directly from the database into a word processing text file is a convenience.

• Availability of content files for the program. The ability to locally adapt or create data files to match the content and level of a course is important. But starting from scratch every time is unnecessarily time consuming if a commercial product is available. Some software producers are marketing data files dealing with various contents. The content of these should be carefully evaluated for accuracy, currency, and level.

• Searching procedures. It is true that the operating procedures vary from one database management program to another, and that the particular commands or procedures needed to manipulate the database must be learned for each different program used. When choosing the management program, select the one which most closely matches the skills being emphasized with the students and the one which will have some carryover to other database applications the students may encounter. If Boolean logic—creating and manipulating sets using the AND and OR connectors—is being stressed with the students, choose a program which allows them to use those connector terms when performing their searches. If students are using an automated card catalog in their library media center which allows Boolean searching, or if they have access to online database searching, choose a database management program which is similar in searching procedures.

• Availability of lab packs. A maximum of two students should work at a computer station for database work. Unlike word processing where one student to one computer is ideal, there is often an advantage to having students team up on this type of thinking activity. For classes of 30 students, 15 copies of the database program must be purchased. Some database programs allow for "multiple boots," but this should be used only if it is in keeping with the intent of the producer's copyright policy.

WHAT COMPUTER HARDWARE IS NEEDED?

After selecting the most appropriate software, hardware considerations are in order. Of critical concern with databases are these hardware factors:

- Memory capacity. Some of the more powerful database management programs require a large portion of computer memory, which then limits the amount of memory available for the database file. The memory capacity of the computers may need to be extended (e.g., from 64K to 128K) to allow the selected program to operate efficiently.
- Disk drives. Some database management programs, such as PFS: File, are operated by first loading the entire program into the computer's memory, and then removing the program disk and inserting the data file disk into the drive. Because the entire management program is in the computer's memory, only the data disk is needed to create, manipulate, or search a data file. This type of system requires only one disk drive. Other programs, such as Appleworks, cannot be entirely loaded into the computer's memory and therefore must be periodically accessed by a drive, going back and forth from the program disk to the file disk. Although it is possible to shuffle the disks in and out of a single drive, it is much more efficient to operate with two disk drives.
- Printers. Some instructional database activities can be carried out without the students having to print out the results of their searches; they simply have to perform the searches and note the results. Other activities require that students print out their search results. The computer lab must be equipped with enough printers that students can do this efficiently. A lab arrangement which includes several computers connected to a printer through a switch box can facilitate the printing process.
- Networking or large-screen display device. Teaching with a database demands frequent modeling, initially when teaching the students the mechanics of using the database, and later when the students are to focus on a particular content or procedure. A computer lab wired with a networking or branching system where a master switch can send a particular screen sequence to each computer monitor accomplishes this focusing

task. A large-screen monitor connected to a single computer could also be used; however, most text is difficult to read on the large monitors. An alternative is a computer video projection device which is connected to the computer and placed on an overhead projector; the text on the computer is converted to a liquid crystal display image on the device, which is then, in turn, enlarged and projected by the overhead. The text is very readable.

Lesson Plans: An Introduction to Databases

The following instructional unit was developed to introduce computerized databases to junior high-age students. The unit was presented by the library media specialist in cooperation with math teachers.

Lesson 1

Materials needed:
- File folder of Student Data Forms (already completed by the students and entered into the Appleworks database management program) (see Figure 8.1).
- File folders of sorted (on several different fields) and printed data from the Appleworks Student Data Base.
- Transparencies
- Overhead projector

Objectives:
- The learner will define database.
- The learner will generate examples of databases.
- The learner will define the following database terms: file, record, field.

Lesson Input:

1. Ask students, "Where do we find information?" Ideas might include: parents, teachers, librarians, doctors, books, television, magazines.
2. Add computers to the list. Tell students, "Computers can store vast amounts of information. The information that we are accustomed to finding in encyclopedias, books, periodical indexes, card catalogs, we can now sometimes find by accessing computers instead. This is an exciting new development for us because not only can a computer store huge amounts of information in a small space, but it is also becoming easier for us to get to the information. The com-

FIGURE 8.1. Student Data Form

```
Last Name _____   First Name _____
Homeroom Teacher_____   Month of Birth _____
Elementary School _____   Age _____   Sex ____
Favorite T.V. Program _____
Favorite Food _____
Number of hours that you watch T.V. each week _____
Number of books that you read in the past month _____
Time for the 1 mile run this fall in P.E. _____
Have you ever broken a bone? (Y or N) _____
Favorite subject (circle 1):
    math    science    global studies    language arts    P.E.    art
    Keyboarding/word processing    home ec.    reading    Spanish
    French    German    health    general music

School clubs or groups to which you currently or plan to belong
(circle up to 5):
    SEEK    debate    yearbook    MathCounts    cheerleading
    chorus    photography    band    orchestra    football
    basketball    volleyball    track    wrestling    student council
    other (please list) _____

Favorite leisure time activities (circle up to 3):
    swimming    boating    biking    loafing    skateboarding
    fishing    reading    watching T.V.    shopping    biking
    other (please list) _____

Favorite type of book (circle 1):
    science fiction    mystery    biography    romance    non-fiction
    fantasy    horror    adventure    teen stories    historical fiction
    humor    other (please list) _____
```

puter gives us better access to the information than we can sometimes get using the standard methods."

3. Introduce the concept of *database*. A database is a collection of information which is presented in a certain format and which can be sorted or arranged. Not all databases are computerized. Ask students to name databases they are familiar with. Examples might include: card catalog, telephone book, dictionary, *TV Guide,* a teacher's grade book. Ask the students to justify their examples against the definition.

4. Tell students, "Although databases do not have to involve computers, there are some advantages to computerizing databases."

5. Introduce the three key database terms: "file," "record," and "field."

6. Show the Student Data Forms, previously completed. Ask the students to label the file, record, and field.

Activity:

1. Distribute folders to groups of students. One group will have a folder that contains all of the forms the students completed. The other groups receive folders that contain computer database printouts of the same information but sorted on different fields. Tell the students that each folder contains the same information. (Do not tell them that it is sorted differently.)
2. Explain that they will be asked questions which they must try to answer as quickly as possible using the information in their folders.
3. Ask questions such as the following. Record which group finished first, second, etc., for each question.
   a. How many students went to Longfellow Elementary school?
   b. How many students are female and went to Hoover Elementary school?
   c. How many students were born in December and list fantasy as their favorite type of book?

Summary:

1. Analyze the results. Ask the students why they could answer some questions more quickly than other questions.
2. Ask the students from each group to describe how the information in their folders was arranged by the computer for them.
3. Ask the students to summarize their findings from the activity: that it is easier and faster for a computer to "shuffle" through forms and sort information than it is for us to do it.

Lesson 2

Materials needed:
- Sets of attribute cards and hoops
- Transparencies
- Overhead projector

Objectives:
- The learner will relate "searching" attribute cards to searching a computer database.
- The learner will demonstrate the effects of using AND and OR in searching multipart questions.

Lesson Input:

1. Show transparency of the Student Data Form. Remind the students of the activity in Lesson 1. Computers are better at sorting through information than we are—they are much faster and more efficient.
2. Review the three database terms from Lesson 1—file, record, and field.
3. Ask students to develop other questions which could be answered by the information in the Student Data Base, pointing out that a complex question is one which focuses on more than one field. Show how the connectors AND and OR link the fields.
4. Discuss what happens with AND and what happens with OR when each is used to connect two fields. Ask questions such as, "Will all students who are 12 raise their hands?" "Will all students who are 13 raise their hands?" "Will all students who are 12 OR 13 raise their hands?" "Will all students who are 12 AND 13 raise their hands?"
5. The OR connector makes the set larger, or expands it. The AND connector makes the set smaller, or limits it. This is the rule in the logic that the computer uses.
6. When searching, the computer will include in the answer set only those items which satisfy both conditions if they are connected with AND. When connected by OR, however, only one of the conditions need be met in order to be included in the answer set.

Activity:

1. Distribute attribute circles and packets of attribute cards to each small group. Explain that the activity will illustrate how a computer deals with the AND and OR connectors when searching. Show on a transparency what attributes the cards have. Ask students to figure out how many cards there are in each packet on the basis of the number of attributes (two sizes times four colors times five shapes).
2. Allow two to three minutes for the students to sort the cards in some way. Remind them that no one way is necessarily right; one characteristic of a database is that it can be sorted in different ways.
3. Ask the students to put all of the rectangle cards in one of the attribute circles and all of the blue cards in the other attribute circle. Let the students discover the question of what to do with the blue rectangles. Suggest that it is necessary to overlap the circles, so that those cards which represent two attributes have a designated area.

4. Give the students several problems: blue triangle; green large; small hexagon. In each problem the students must first place the cards in the appropriate places relative to the attribute circles—in either one circle or the other, in the overlapped area, or outside both circles. Next the students must be able to describe each section of the circles using precise language. "This area is blue. This area is triangle. This area is blue and triangle. This area is blue or triangle. This area is red or yellow or green and rectangle or circle or hexagon or square." (see Figure 8.2.)

FIGURE 8.2. Attribute Card Activity

Summary:

1. Apply this type of logic to the "attributes" involved in the class database. Tell the students that when the computer is asked to find those students who went to Longfellow School and were born in February, it will not count the Longfellow students who were born in the other 11 months, nor will it count the students born in February who went to other

schools. Draw attribute circles and label them for Long-fellow and February.

2. Ask the students to illustrate other database questions by drawing and labeling attribute circles.

Lesson 3

Materials needed:
- Large poster showing various attributes (color, size, shape, texture)
- A computer system plus one large-screen monitor
- HighWire Logic (software package) from Sunburst
- "slide show disks" selected from HighWire Logic

Objectives:
- The learner will relate the more abstract sets shown on a computer screen to the manipulative sets used in Lesson 2.
- The learner will define a given set using the proper Boolean connectors (AND or OR).

Lesson Input:

1. Introduce HighWire Logic. A prepared "slide show" of selected screens from the program will facilitate this. It will allow for planned, carefully selected examples to demonstrate to the students how to attack the problems. Explain that students must develop statements using the attributes and the connector words to describe the sets generated by the program (see Figure 8.3).

FIGURE 8.3. Instruction with AND/OR Connectors using HighWire Logic

Used by permission of Sunburst Communications Inc., Pleasantville, NY.

2. Show a screen which explains how the AND connector works. Then show several problems, guiding the students to describe the sets using attribute words and the connnector AND.

3. Show a screen which explains how the OR connector works. Then show several problems, guiding the students to describe the sets using attribute words and the connector OR.

4. As each HighWire problem appears, call on students to suggest statements. Type in their statements. Encourage students to come up with as many statements for each problem as possible. Appropriate questions to guide the students include: "What do you see?" "Why do you think that statement will work?" "How did you figure that out?" This approach may help others to pick up on a strategy or pattern.

FIGURE 8.4. Using Computer Logic to search Appleworks Database

Lesson 4

Materials needed:
- Computer lab with two students per station
- Computer with liquid crystal projection device
- Overhead projector
- Appleworks software for each station
- Data disks for each station
—Student worksheets

Objectives:

- The learner will learn to operate the Appleworks database system.
- The learner will search a database to find information.
- The learner will perform AND and OR searches.

Lesson input:

1. Using the computer with an attached projection device, demonstrate how to manipulate the Appleworks database: how to select from the menu, and how to select records to perform specified searches (see Figure 8.4).
2. Work through several problems together.
3. Instruct students to work through the remainder of the questions with their computer partner, recording the answers on their worksheets.

REFERENCES

Hodson, Yvonne D. and David Leibelshon. "Creating Databases with Students." *School Library Journal* 32 (May 1986): LC12–15.

Hunter, Beverly. "Problem Solving with Databases." *The Computing Teacher* 12 (May 1985): 20–27.

Naisbitt, John. *Megatrends.* New York: Warner, 1982.

Olds, Henry F. "Information Management: A New Tool for a New Curriculum." *Computers in the Schools* 3 (1986): 7–22.

Roszak, Theodore. *The Cult of Information.* New York: Pantheon, 1986.

Schiffman, Shirl S. "Productivity Tools for the Classroom." *The Computing Teacher* 13 (May 1986): 27–31.

Thomas, Rick. "The Student-Designed Database." *The Computing Teacher* 15 (February 1988): 17–19.

White, Charles S. "Developing Information-Processing Skills through Structured Activities with a Computerized File-Management Program." *Journal of Educational Computing Research* 3 (1987): 355–75.

SOFTWARE REFERENCES

Appleworks. Apple Computer, Inc., Cupertino, CA.

Bank Street Filer. Scholastic, Inc., Jefferson City, MO.

Beginning Bank Street Filer. Scholastic, Inc., Jefferson City, MO.

Bookworm. Minnesota Educational Computing Consortium, St. Paul, MN.

HighWire Logic. Sunburst Communications, Pleasantville, NY.

PFS: File. Scholastic, Inc., Jefferson City, MO.

Chapter 9
Information Skills

The school library media program has a curriculum of skills to be taught. While those skills are most effectively taught by integrating the instruction into content addressed by classroom teachers, still there is an identifiable body of information skills to which the school library media specialist is committed to teaching.

Those skills have focused on location of information in specific sources. Note the terms "location" and "sources." It is these two focal points that are likely to change as library media specialists begin to prepare students for an information age in which technology changes how to access information and in which the vastness of the information base forces a shift in emphasis from locating to evaluating information. Traditional library skills have concentrated on how to use an index, how to use a card catalog, and how to locate items on library shelves on the basis of call numbers. While these skills are valid for libraries of today, technology is rapidly changing how indexes work, what card catalogs look like, and whether to locate information on a shelf or on a screen or printout. Forward-looking library curriculum designers are reassessing the content of the library media curriculum.

A card catalog typifies a manual index system taught in most school library media programs. The system is based on subject headings determined by some authority, usually Sears or the Library of Congress. Students must learn to work within the parameters of that subject access system; one skill to be acquired in such a system is the use of "see" and "see also" cross-references. In addition, the search for combined subjects like alcoholism and teenagers is awkward at best in such a system, and students often look up several subject headings, locating some amount of irrelevant information before arriving at just the right items. Yet students are applying the information skills appropriate to the manual search. Technology is bringing to students new methods of searching for information. Along with that comes the need for new information search skills. Besides subject headings, students must master the concept of keywords to perform automated searches. Use of related terms and Boolean operators help students to broaden and narrow searches. And so, teaching how to design a search strategy to maximize the power of automated databases and to key in on specific and relevant information becomes a critical skill.

There has been a tendency to teach students sources of information: "Where do you find the names of state capitals?" "Where do you find annual average rainfall by country?" "Where do you find biographical data on famous Americans still living?" However, instead of focusing on specific sources, it is the process of information seeking which is essential for students to learn. Part of that process is question formulation. The student must ask the question. Student experiences can include the process of question development, particularly if library media instruction is integrated into classroom curriculum content. What skills do students need to learn? Clearly, many of the skills currently taught continue to be appropriate; the concepts of keyword and index and the skill of narrowing a topic continue to have relevance. Yet, there are additional skills and concepts which are emerging as important for today's students: formulating a sound search strategy, using Boolean logic to define topics, selecting relevant information, comparing information from various sources, sorting our extraneous information, validating information, recognizing self-interest in information sources. These additional skills and concepts emerge as a result of the increased availability of information and the increased accessibility afforded by automated information systems. These added skills represent considerable emphasis on processes of accessing and using information and less emphasis on locating within specific sources. Another change in emphasis represented here is a move to teach not only how to find information but also what to do with it once found. The highly touted information explosion is forcing us to become more selective and evaluative as we look at the wealth of information available today. So, looking at reliability of sources, at currency of information, and at substantiation of arguments becomes critical in dealing with information overload. These are important additions to the information skill curriculum.

Several leaders in school librarianship are addressing this issue. Betty Cleaver (1987) raises the issue that students need opportunities to think about information itself. She suggests students be confronted with such questions as: "What kinds of information do we need to make decisions?" "Does the medium of information change the content?" She suggests that the ethics of using information will be a critical issue for students as the automated manipulation of text facilitates the "borrowing" of words of others. Carol Kuhlthau (1987) suggests a philosophical shift in library instruction. She urges a move away from a source approach centering on students learning to use their particular library and its specific sources toward a process approach. This approach places a great deal of emphasis on defining the information problem at the front end and analyzing the results of the search at the back end. In source-based library instruction the emphasis has been on the middle steps of the process, on the locating of information instead of on the questioning and evaluating which are emphasized in a process approach. The process approach depends for its success on library instruction being fully integrated into classroom learning, so that the problem definition and the information evaluation have adequate context to be important. Isolated library exercises won't matter enough and won't have enough consequence for the student.

Jacqueline Mancall and others (1986) likewise call for a move to greater attention to process and less attention to specific sources. David Loertscher (1984) has identified several information skills to be added to the K-12 curriculum. He has outlined those skills emphasizing the ability to formulate a sound search strategy to find information and the ability to deal with the results of an information search. In addition, he has identified a number of thinking skills to be addressed in the information searching process. Loertscher suggests that databases provide an excellent instructional vehicle for teaching these information skills, with online searching as a valuable and practical experience.

The collected wisdom of these library media leaders tells us that the processes of information gathering and use are changing; today's student will solve information problems in new, more efficient and perhaps more scientific ways.

When confronted with an information need or problem to solve, the student of the traditional curriculum would attack the problem by seeking information, analyzing the information, and communicating the results. The tools this student used in solving the problem might include pencil and paper for recording, collating, and arranging the information; a calculator to explore statistical relationships; graph paper to illustrate the results; and a typewriter to explain the results. But in schools where technological change has been embraced, students can learn to make connections with information in different ways. Computer technology offers students a means to address problems and, therefore, the process of working with information (Hoelscher 1986). Databases, spreadsheets, word processors, and graphics generators are the new tools a student can use to attack a problem.

Regardless of whether "manual" tools or computer tools are used, the same problem or informational need is explored, perhaps even resulting in the same outcome. It is the process of working with information which has been changed by technology, and while the end results may not be different, the student's depth of understanding may be enhanced. Technology empowers the student to look at information in many more ways, accessing it more precisely, exploring it from different angles, restructuring it, all before deciding how to communicate the results. Because technology is changing the nature of information processing, students must learn to use the electronic tools which drive our information society.

In Chapter 8 the instructional use of databases was described. By using a database with students, a teacher has the opportunity to focus on several higher-order thinking skills, such as comparing, drawing inferences, and hypothesizing, and has yet another instructional strategy for imparting information to the students. At the same time the students are learning skills essential to locating and manipulating information in our increasingly technology-driven society.

The computerized database is at the heart of information management; the library media specialist is responsible for teaching students information management. Therefore, understanding what a database is and how it works and being proficient in manipulating one are core skills of a library media program.

This is not to say that "old-fashioned" library skills should not be taught. Most library resources will be around for some time in the same form they are in now, and librarians and library users need to be aware of them and how to use them to find information. Most of us could pull Bartlett's *Familiar Quotations* from the reference shelf and find out who wrote that poem about the purple cow faster than we could check some online or CD-ROM reference tool. And while *Books in Print* online provides a convenient service to librarians, it is rather costly for any extended period of searching.

In *The Cult of Information,* Theodore Roszak (1986) writes that he found librarians very helpful, performing online database searches for him which yielded more materials than he would have found doing the computer searches himself. The librarians were better at searching because they were more familiar with the various databases and more efficient with the searching procedures and strategies.

But Roszak also found the librarians helpful when they knew enough not to use the computer for finding the information. "Librarians know what many dedicated hackers overlook: as an information-processing instrument, the computer supplements other sources, it does not replace them" (Roszak, 174).

When databases are used instructionally by classroom teachers in various fields such as science or social studies, the focus is generally on the content and analysis of the content. Databases in the library media center have a different focus. Here the database is used as a tool for locating, and in some instances processing, information.

Students need to master specific skills in order to use various library media center tools. Using the card catalog requires that students understand alphabetizing rules, subject headings, and cross references. Using a periodical index requires that they understand subject headings and subheadings, cross-references, and citation abbreviations and formats.

Using a computerized database requires that the students understand essentially these same skills, but to take full advantage of the power of the computer, they must also understand the concepts of keyword searching and Boolean connectors. It is in the skillful use of these two techniques that the true potency of a computerized database is realized.

What follows is a description of the information gathering process a student would go through when researching a topic in a contemporary library media center, taking advantage of traditional information-yielding resources as well as newer, technology-driven resources.

When flashy, high-tech sources are available, it is tempting to bypass those worn volumes shelved in most reference collections, but it is nevertheless important for students to check the available conventional tools. One reason for this is that by perusing reference books, a student can develop a finer focus or scope for the topic being researched. Browsing through a manual encyclopedia or periodical index allows the student to see relationships within or between subjects. This is not as easily accomplished when working at a terminal where there is only a window view of the information. Another rationale for performing manual searches is that the student can begin to build up a bank of appropriate descriptors (subject headings) relating to the topic which will be useful when accessing computerized resources.

A *research checklist* such as that shown in Figure 9.1 serves as map for the student in maneuvering through the research process. It reminds the student of the available resources in the library media center, encouraging thorough, exhaustive research; it also reminds the student to record relevant descriptors discovered while researching the topic.

After deciding on a possible topic, the student lists the keywords which will serve as the initial access points to information on the topic. "The Growing Problem of Alcohol Abuse among Teenagers" contains the keywords "alcohol" and "teenagers."

The student begins the information search by checking the indexes of various general and specialized reference books for citations relating to "alcohol" and "teenagers." Cross-references mentioned are recorded on the checklist as possible descriptors. For example, the encyclopedia index may employ a "see" reference from "teenagers" to "juveniles" or "adolescents," or a "see also" reference from "alcohol" to "alcohol abuse" to "substance abuse."

Armed with these descriptors the student is now ready to perform an automated search of a similar type of information source— *The Electronic Encyclopedia,* Grolier's CD-ROM version of the *Aca-*

FIGURE 9.1. Research Checklist

Make a working bibliography as you check each source. Record descriptors you discover.

___ **Reference Collection**   **Descriptors**

Check the indexes of general and   _____
specific reference tools. Use   _____
subject headings and cross-references.   _____

___ **Electronic Encyclopedia**

Perform keyword searches. Use   _____
descriptors as keywords. Use   _____
Boolean connectors.   _____

___ **General Collection**

Check the catalog for print and   _____
nonprint resources. Use subject   _____
headings and cross-references.   _____

___ **Readers' Guide to Periodical Literature**

Check each available issue. Use   _____
subject headings and cross-references.   _____
                                             _____
                                             _____
                                             _____

___ **Online Database**

Perform keyword searches. Use   _____
descriptors as keywords. Use   _____
Boolean connectors.   _____
                                             _____

demic American Encyclopedia. CD-ROM stands for "compact disk read-only memory." The information is stored and read differently on CD-ROM disks than it is on floppy or hard disks, allowing for much greater storage capacity (McGinty 1987). The entire text of the 20-volume encyclopedia set is stored on one CD-ROM disk, actually occupying only about one-tenth of the disk's storage capacity. An extensive indexing system, occupying another one-tenth of the disk, allows the user to quickly search for the occurrences of virtually every word of the encyclopedia (Vandergrift 1987).

What is the advantage of using this computerized encyclopedia over its paper counterpart? The power is in its full-text, keyword, and Boolean searching capabilities. An encyclopedia article is assigned a very limited number of subject headings which appear in the printed index. This means that potentially relevant information often goes undetected by a student researcher because it is buried away in an article without adequate indexing. Statistics on alcohol abuse among teenagers may be included as a comparison point within an article on marijuana. With limited indexing, the researcher is not given a clue to this potential information, and may not think to check the marijuana article, thereby missing the statistics. In the full-text searching process of a CD-ROM encyclopedia the alcohol statistics would have been located, for when the descriptor "alcohol" is entered, the entire encyclopedia database is searched for every occurrence of the word "alcohol" regardless in which article it is mentioned.

Keyword searching also overcomes a limitation of traditional indexing. When using the index volume of an encyclopedia, the researcher must express the topic in the established vocabulary of the indexers, and must thread carefully through the cross-references to successfully locate the desired information. Keyword searching opens this process up dramatically, accepting a much broader range of descriptors.

Finally, the CD-ROM encyclopedia allows for Boolean searching techniques which can streamline searching of multiconcept topics. It is relatively simple to search an encyclopedia index for information on a single topic such as "alcohol"; it is a much more complex task to search that index for information on "alcohol," but only as it relates to or involves "teenagers." This task requires the researcher to juggle both topics, checking under both subject headings, often having to skim the articles themselves to determine if there is indeed present the specific information. The Boolean searching capabilities of a computerized database, coupled with keyword searching, allow the student to develop a search statement linking the topics appropriately. The computer then performs the search as specified, juggling the topics much more efficiently than could be handled in a manual search. The search statement of "alcohol AND (teenagers OR adolescents)" will yield articles which contain information about alcohol relating to young people. The resulting articles can be skimmed, and additional searches either broader or narrower in scope can be performed.

The next step of the research process is to locate the print and nonprint resources available in the general collection of the library media center. The catalog, whether a traditional card catalog or an automated catalog, serves as the index to the collection. The type of searching procedure used in accessing the catalog depends on its format. If it is a card catalog, searching is performed by subject heading and cross-reference checking; if it is an automated catalog, keyword and Boolean searching may be possible.

An automated catalog has some of the same advantages over a traditional card catalog that the CD-ROM encyclopedia has over its print counterpart. While "full-text" searching of each document in the catalog is not possible, keyword searching on any or all fields in the catalog database is a powerful option. Again, a print index offers a limited number of subject headings assigned to each item. A videotape on "Issues Facing Teens Today" may not have "alcohol" assigned as a subject heading in a card catalog although it is one of the many topics discussed. In an automated catalog containing records in MARC format, a search on the keyword "alcohol" would locate all occurrences of the word whether in the title or subject fields, as well as in the annotation field. Also, Boolean searching capabilities in an automated catalog allow the student to search multiconcept topics more efficiently. Finally, some powerful, sophisticated, automated catalog systems allow for networking—granting the user bibliographic access not only to the holdings of the on-site library collection, but also to the holdings of other collections, perhaps other schools in the district or area, perhaps the local public library. With interlibrary loan agreements in place, access to information can be greatly increased for the student.

To locate relevant periodical articles, the student researcher systematically checks each available issue of *Readers' Guide to Periodical Literature,* again noting the various descriptors which apply to the subject. Even though an online database search will be performed to provide more current, comprehensive access to periodical articles, there is nevertheless value in checking a topic in a manual periodical index. Besides suggesting additional descriptors, the index can offer a browsing searcher the "big picture" of how related topics hang together, which can be useful when trying to fine-tune an online search. It is necessary for the student to approach this print index from several angles in order to find the relevant articles on a multiple-concept topic, making use of sub-headings and cross-references.

Performing an online database search is the next step of the research process. Online database searching has been available for more than 20 years in the academic world. This research tool is now becoming more common at the intermediate and secondary school levels because of: (1) the proliferation of databases, including many which are appropriate, relevant, and useful to the general public and school-age students; (2) the simplification of searching techniques, with protocols and language becoming more natural and logical in "human" terms; and (3) the diminishing costs involved. The cost of the necessary hardware is becoming manageable by most schools, and many information vendors, jumping at the opportunity to gain more consumers, are offering reduced online rates for student searching, as well as developing materials to be used with the students in teaching them online searching skills. This is a smart marketing strategy on the part of the vendors: the earlier students learn and see the value of online database searching, the more readily they will turn to it when confronted with an informational need in the future.

Of all the technological developments appearing on the library information retrieval scene, online database searching is probably the most feasible for the lowest initial financial outlay. The cost of converting a card catalog to an automated catalog with full MARC records and keyword and Boolean searching capabilities may be out of the reach of some schools. Likewise, the cost of the new hardware involved in CD-ROM technology may be prohibitive right now for some school library budgets. But even a very small school can fund the start-up costs involved in going online. Most schools already have at least some of the components necessary to begin online searching: a microcomputer with disk drives and printer, and a telephone line. Also necessary are a modem, which converts computer signals to telephone signals; telecommunications software, which facilitates the dialogue between the user's computer and the remote database computer; and an account with one or more online vendors such as DIALOG, BRS, and WILSONLINE (Tenopir 1986). The modem and telecommunications software should be selected carefully so that they are compatible to each other and easily perform the functions particularly critical to online searching. Various articles have been published recently which address the selecting of appropriate modems and software.

Before going online, the student researcher must complete a *Search Strategy Worksheet* to ensure that the search is well thought out (see Figure 9.2). The student should always have a plan when researching, but this becomes more crucial when researching online because of the hourly cost of access. Part of the Search Strategy Worksheet asks the student to develop alternate search statements to use in the event that the search does not yield the anticipated results (e.g., too many citations, too few citations).

Online periodical databases have several advantages over manual periodical indexes. More recent articles are found using an online service because the databases are updated more frequently than traditional indexes. There is a wide array of databases available to the searcher, extending much broader and more comprehensive periodical indexing than a typical school library media center could afford to offer.

Online searching makes use of keyword and Boolean strategies, but most databases do not, as yet, offer full-text searching. This means that the computer searches the database for the desired keyword in various fields such as the title and author fields, the annotation field, and the descriptor fields (similar to the subject

FIGURE 9.2. Search Strategy Worksheet

TOPIC: *The growing problem of (alcohol) abuse among (teenagers)*

Circle keywords or descriptors. Add here other descriptors that you found that explain or relate to your topic.

alcoholism	*youth*
drinking	*juveniles*
substance abuse	*children*
drug abuse	*adolescents*

Using Boolean operators, connect your keywords or descriptors into a SEARCH STATEMENT. Circle the connectors.

alcohol (AND) (teenagers (OR) adolescents)

Using the connector AND, change your SEARCH STATEMENT to narrow the search. Use this statement if the original SEARCH STATEMENT results in too many hits.

alcohol (AND) (teenagers (OR) adolescents) (AND) rural

Using the connector OR, change your SEARCH STATEMENT to broaden the search. Use this statement if the original SEARCH STATEMENT results in too few hits.

(alcohol (OR) drug) (AND) (teenagers (OR) adolescents (OR) children (OR) youth)

headings on a catalog card), but the entire article is not searched for an occurrence of the keyword—at least not in most databases.

Boolean searching is a powerful tool for connecting keywords in multiconcept topics to create new sets. "Alcohol OR alcoholism OR alcohol abuse" will yield a large number of citations in a general periodical database. "Teenagers OR adolescents" will also yield many citations. When the two sets are joined by the connector AND, the number of citations will decrease, the new set eliminating those articles about alcohol but not about young people and those articles about teens but not about alcohol. If the search still yields too many citations, it can be narrowed further by combining the set with another using the Boolean AND or by using NOT to exclude a certain keyword. If the search is too narrow, if the original search yields too few citations, it can be broadened by connecting additional descriptors with the Boolean OR.

At this point the information-gathering process a student undertakes when researching a topic is complete. The student has searched for relevant information in a variety of traditional library resources as well as some technology-driven resources, the outcome of the search being a working bibliography—a list of citations of encyclopedia articles, periodical articles, and print and nonprint resources in the library media center collection. But locating the information is only one part of the information processing picture.

Jerry McClelland (1986) writes that students need to possess two essential skills to cope in our information society: the ability to search computer databases and the ability to use information in decision making to solve a problem. This second skill is significantly more complex, involving higher levels of cognition such as analysis and evaluation. McClelland has developed a model for information processing as part of a decision-making process.

In a research activity, the "problem" confronting a student is locating appropriate information to present relevant facts or support a thesis. After researching the topic and compiling a bibliography of potential sources, the student must assess the relevance and validity of the information. Anyone who has done any online database searching knows that most searches yield some, and some searches yield massive amounts of, irrelevant information. Experienced searchers strive for high recall (finding all the available relevant information—not "missing something good") and also high precision (having a high percentage of relevant articles from all those retrieved—not "catching a lot of junk"). With student searchers it is generally preferable to go for high recall while searching, then sort out the irrelevant "junk" manually, later.

Evaluating the validity of information sources is difficult to teach. Students must learn to question the sources and eliminate those which are not appropriate. Is the information current enough to be valid? Is the information logical and consistent with other facts? Is the information understandable by the student? Even when searching a general-interest database, such as *Magazine Index,* some citations may be to articles too advanced for a young student to comprehend. A junior high student looking for information on AIDS will have better success in understanding an article in a magazine such as *Time* or *Health* than one in *The New England Journal of Medicine.*

Another difficult step is determining if there is enough information or if more is needed. If gaps are discovered, the student should go back and conduct additional searches of various sources. Finally, the student must try to judge the relative importance of the various bits of information found. This is a very subjective task, but one which can greatly influence the outcome of the research process.

Now, the information processing model is complete (see Figure 9.3). The student has identified and addressed an information need, located sources of appropriate information, and evaluated the information.

FIGURE 9.3. Research Model

Identify the Informational Need	Locate Sources of Information	Evaluate the Information
Use standard reference books to develop focus or scope	Use indexes of general and specific reference tools	Assess relevancy
		Assess validity
	Perform keyword search of an electronic encyclopedia	Assess appropriateness
Determine relationships between and within subjects		
Develop descriptors (list of keywords)	Use card catalog or automated catalog to locate print and nonprint resources	
	Use Readers' Guide to Periodical Literature	
	Perform online data base search	

SUMMARY

The computer can become an important tool in the search for information. With an exploding worldwide database confronting us, we must find ways to sift out that which can answer the questions we have. That sifting process requires identifiable skills, and today's schools must be addressing those skills. Effective information searching begins with formulating questions. Next comes designing a search strategy to plan a pathway through the various indexes and sources available to us, whether they are manual or computerized aids. This search strategy step requires some important subskills related to broadening or narrowing a search using accurate keywords and Boolean operators to combine them. Once sources are located, specific criteria must be applied to evaluate them; that evaluation must be associated with the initial goal of the searcher. Finally, the searcher must be able to evaluate the importance of the information found. This list of steps represents a curriculum somewhat different from that which currently exists in many schools. It is the responsibility of educators to provide today's students with those skills needed to be effective consumers of information.

REFERENCES

Cleaver, Betty. "Thinking about Information: Skills for Lifelong Learning." *School Library Media Quarterly* 15 (Fall 1987): 29–31.

Hoelscher, Karen. "Computing and Information: Steering Student Learning." *Computers in the Schools* 3 (1986): 23–24.

Kuhlthau, Carol. "An Emerging Theory of Library Instruction." *School Library Media Quarterly* 15 (Fall, 1987): 23–28.

Loertscher, David V. "Information Skills for Children and Young Adults: Start Now!" *School Library Media Activities Monthly* 1 (December 1984): 30–34.

McClelland, Jerry. "A Twist on an Old Skill: Retrieving Information with Computers to Enhance Decision-Making Processes." *Computers in the Schools* 3 (1986): 83–88.

McGinty, Tony. "Three Trailblazing Technologies for Schools." *Electronic Learning* 7 (September 1987): 26–30.

Mancall, Jacqueline C., Shirley L. Aaron and Sue A. Walker. "Educating Students to Think: The Role of the School Library Media Program." *School Library Media Quarterly* 15 (Fall 1986): 18–27.

Roszak, Theodore. *The Cult of Information.* New York: Pantheon, 1986.

Tenopir, Carol. "Student Online Database Searching, Part 1." *The Computing Teacher* 13 (April 1986): 18–19.

Vandergrift, Kay E., Marlyn Kemper, Sandra Champion and Jane Anne Hannigan. "CD-ROM: Perspectives on an Emerging Technology." *School Library Journal* 33 (June–July 1987): 27–31.

SOFTWARE REFERENCES

BRS. Latham, NY.

DIALOG Information Services. Palo Alto, CA.

WILSONLINE. Bronx, NY.

Chapter 10
Using the Computer to Teach Thinking Skills

The teaching of thinking is of great concern in schools today. Teachers in mathematics, English, social science, science, and the arts all recognize the need for developing in students the ability to analyze, classify, compare, hypothesize, and infer. These cognitive skills are critical for young people facing a world of information overload. While there was a time when curriculum was concerned with covering content, the idea of content emphasis becomes impossible when the amount of information available within any discipline is far beyond what can be covered. So it becomes increasingly important that students gain skill in how to process information. It is these thought process skills which constitute important content for today's schools.

A critical point of emphasis throughout this book has been the importance of identifying what can be taught better with the computer than with other media. The concern for teaching students the process of thinking presents an excellent opportunity to use the medium of the computer. The computer and appropriate software can help the teacher to create a closed microcosm with little distraction from subject area content. Instead of content, process becomes the focus.

LOGO

LOGO represents one attempt at creating an environment in which such a focus on process can occur. While the jury is still out on the effectiveness of LOGO in developing problem-solving skills and particularly on the transfer of LOGO learnings to other problem-solving situations, clearly LOGO-philes express enthusiasm with the events they experience with children (Rieber 1987). There are, however, some very practical concerns to be addressed in considering LOGO as a strategy for teaching problem solving. One of those concerns is teacher training. In our experience, a minimum of 40 hours of initial teacher training was offered for teachers to begin to implement LOGO in their classrooms. This is a heavy time commitment for teachers. Furthermore, certain elementary teachers have more aptitude than others for facilitating LOGO in their classrooms; teachers who tend to be analytical in their own thought processes seem much more able to facilitate students in LOGO. It seems critical to the success of LOGO at the elementary level that the teacher have the option to choose LOGO or some other strategy to address problem-solving skills. In addition, computer access must be considered. Each student needs daily access to a computer in order to experiment and test; at this time rather few public elementary schools are equipped to provide long enough periods of one-to-one computer access for whole classes of students daily. Another practical consideration is the school day schedule. Again, rather few public schools today are willing to displace a substantial segment of the ongoing math program to provide enough instructional time for children to get to high enough levels of LOGO to become complex problem solvers. Decision makers do well to consider all practical factors before committing teacher and student time and resources to the adoption of LOGO as a problem-solving strategy.

PROBLEM-SOLVING SOFTWARE

Another approach to using the computer to teach problem solving and thinking is to identify effective software and use it in a demonstration mode, one computer for a whole class (see Figure 10.1). An example of that is a program from The Learning Company entitled Moptown Parade (see Figure 10.2). Level 6 of the program's content centers on creating a parade of imaginary characters called "Gribbits" and "Bibbits." Its intent is to involve some specific thinking skills of classifying, comparing, and contrasting. To teach those thinking skills using, for example, science content forces students to spend time learning about science, and the process may get short shrift.

Focusing on the processes with the computer allows students to develop those skills and then apply them as strategies as they later think about science. The teacher must make the decision about whether to introduce the content first and then the thinking skill (or process to be used in manipulating the content), or whether to teach the thinking skill first and then apply that skill as the content is introduced. There is no one right way. The point is that when the focus on process is important, there needs to be a vehicle for addressing that. The computer and accompanying thinking skill software provide a solution.

Selecting the software is a critical decision. In Figure 10.3, there are examples of programs and the targeted thinking skills addressed.

FIGURE 10.1. Teaching Problem Solving to an Entire Class

FIGURE 10.2. Moptown Parade, The Learning Company

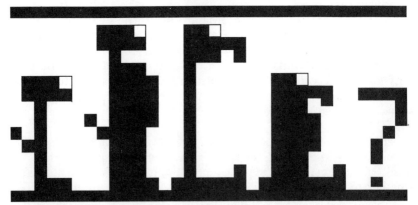

WHO COMES NEXT?
TALL OR SHORT? (T OR S)

Reprinted with permission from The Learning Company, Fremont, CA. Copyright, Leslie Grimm, The Learning Company 979-643.

FIGURE 10.3. Thinking Skills Software

Program	Targeted Skills
Blockers and Finders (Sunburst)	inferences
The Factory (Sunburst)	spatial relations, multiple solutions
The Incredible Laboratory (Sunburst)	hypothesizing, data organization
Safari Search (Sunburst)	deductive reasoning, inferences
The King's Rule (Sunburst)	inductive reasoning
Moptown Parade (Learning Company)	critical attributes, comparing, contrasting
High Wire Logic (Sunburst)	Boolean logic

Questions to ask as one is considering software for teaching thinking skills are:

- Does the software focus on significant and relevant thinking skills?
- Are there multiple levels of difficulty so that the teacher can adjust to students' needs?
- Is the teacher able to control the level at which the group is working?
- Does the software have multiple problems so that it can be used repeatedly?
- Is the software designed for a cooperative rather than competitive environment?
- Are the graphics clean enough to be displayed effectively on a large-screen monitor?

The design of the software should allow the teacher to focus on a thinking skill or strategy without the gaming or content aspects of the software intruding.

THE TEACHER'S ROLE

What does the teacher do with the software, once identified? Much of the thinking skills software available can be trivialized into a simple game if students are turned loose on their own to sit at the computer and simply try to accomplish a task. A good example of that is a program entitled The Incredible Laboratory from Sunburst (see Figure 10.4). Students working alone can play the game and create monsters. However, they may or may not be able to discuss a strategy for controlling the outcome or controlling variables. In short, they have played their way to a solution. This approach to the use of problem-solving software assumes that the answer is the important issue when in fact the process of getting the solution is the important issue. To ensure focus on process, the teacher, not the computer and not the student, must be in charge.

FIGURE 10.4. The Incredible Laboratory

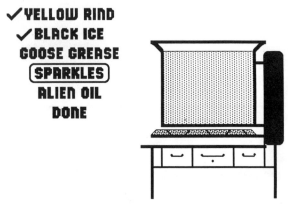

Used by permission of Sunburst Communications, Inc., Pleasantville, NY.

In the arena of thinking skills, teachers, not computers, teach (van Deusen and Donham 1987). So, what does it look like for a teacher to be "in charge?" One arrangement that works well is for the computer to be connected to a large-screen color monitor. The teacher is then in charge of the keyboard and thus in charge of the proceedings. The teacher uses the computer as a teaching medium just as he or she might use a chalk board. The computer's interactive capability and its graphics make it an improvement over chalk. Another factor in using the computer in this way is a method to keep track of students' hypotheses or to label the screen. Stick-on tags are a useful aid for attaching ideas to the screen or for titling rows and columns of matrixes.

In order to teach thinking skills, a critical factor is the creation of an appropriate environment. Roles change also. The teacher's posture moves to the students' side as the computer becomes the player who says "yes" or "no" as feedback to queries. The teacher begins to speak in "we" language: "What should we do next?" "Why should we try that answer?" "How do we know that is a good answer?"

The teacher's language changes as he or she asks questions in order to stimulate thinking (van Deusen 1988). The teacher's response behavior also changes. The teacher must not cue students to stop thinking, but rather encourage more thinking among everyone.

Teacher responses such as "Right," "No," "That's a good idea," "That's close," tend to stifle further thought because students know whether they have said what the teacher wants to hear and so the motivation to keep thinking and searching dies. Instead, the teacher should use statements like: "Why do you think that?" "How do we know that?" "Does everyone agree?" "Can we be sure that will work?" "What else could work?" Each of these statements encourages more thought. The issue of teacher response behaviors has been a topic addressed widely in the literature. Art Costa (1985) among others has suggested teacher responses that seem to facilitate thinking:

- Silence
- Accepting the student's idea: "Do we agree?"
- Integrating the student's idea into previous ideas: "Is one way better than another?"
- Clarifying: "Do you mean. . .?"

Another very effective strategy is to allow students to work collaboratively to come up with an idea, particularly when individually they seem to have "hit the wall" in proposing a reasonable answer or strategy. By saying, "Talk about it in small groups for two minutes," the teacher is reducing the risk of error for individuals and creating a potentially successful situation for students. Such teacher behavior can help to create a stress-free, cooperative classroom environment where experimental ideas can be risked, alternatives explored, and answers changed given added data, and where more value is placed on the thinking strategy than on right answers.

LESSON DESIGN

Lesson designs for using software to teach thinking skills can be divided into three parts. First, the teacher and students work together to try to induce the objective and the rules of the software. That segment of the lesson can begin with a general question like "Let's look at this program and see if we can figure out what we are supposed to do and what the rules are?" At the end of this segment of the lesson, students should be able to state the objective and state the instructions. Why shouldn't the teacher simply give them the rules and proceed into the program itself? One event that occurs during this process is that the students see the teacher move from judge to participant. This is the opportunity for the teacher to begin to work with students as a member of their team while the computer is seen as the problem poser. The camaraderie that is created between teacher and students will be very important for freeing students to think without anxiety about right and wrong answers. Not only are students learning the rules of the program, but they are also learning the rules of the classroom when the computer joins the scene. And they are learning those rules before the instructional focus on a specific thinking skill begins.

After teacher and students have agreed on the rules of the program and the goal and have successfully accomplished the objective of the program once, it is time to challenge students to really think. One way to do this is to add constraints to the process. For example, in Gertrude's Puzzles from The Learning Company, one of the puzzles is a loop puzzle. Two intersecting loops appear on the screen. Puzzle pieces are geometric shapes (triangles, circles, diamonds, etc.) in various colors (see Figure 10.5). Students are challenged to determine the attributes, i.e., color and shape, critical to allowing a piece to stay in a loop or to be dropped from it. The teacher may say, "Let's try to identify the rule for what is in and what is out of the two loops in as few steps as possible." Now, students not only have to find the solution, but have to find it as efficiently as possible.

FIGURE 10.5. Gertrude's Puzzles, The Learning Company

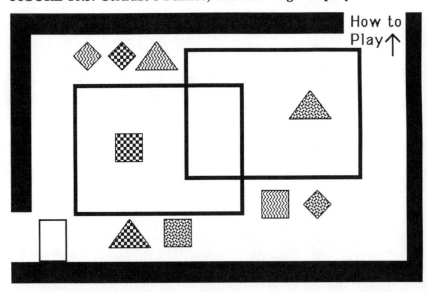

Reprinted with permission from The Learning Company, Fremont, CA. Copyright, The Learning Company 2-219-567.

This situation leads to a series of "what if" questions on the part of the teacher as students struggle to determine what strategy will allow them to eliminate as many extraneous guesses as possible on the way to the solution. The teacher may need to chart the possible outcomes for a variety of "If–then" proposals before a single guess is made on the computer, so that students can be confident they have found a good strategy. This kind of predictive thinking is one important goal in schools today. The computer allows us to create a problem with which to practice such thinking and provides a means to immediately test our thinking.

The third step in the lesson is the statement of the algorithm for the fastest or best solution to the problem. That is a logical sequence of steps stated in language to communicate the best way to solve the problem. That algorithm can only come as a result of a process of hypothesizing, testing, and refining, in an environment where people are thinking aloud and feeling free to try out ideas. In Level 3 of Safari Search from Sunburst, students are confronted with a 5 x 5 grid. A seal is hiding in one of the 25 cells. The goal is to locate the seal. After the students choose a cell location, feedback provided is the number of cells the seal is away via the shortest nondiagonal path from the cell chosen. The algorithm for finding the seal in the fewest number of moves is to choose one of the four corner cells. The possible locations for the seal form a diagonal line zero to eight cells away from the cell chosen. If the next move is either of the two adjacent corners to the first cell chosen, another diagonal line of cells, perpendicular to the first line, can be drawn. Only one cell will be common to the two diagonal lines. That common cell must contain the seal (see Figure 10.6).

QUESTIONING

Teacher questions, as well as teacher responses to students, can have substantial impact on the kind of thinking that occurs (Ornstein 1987). Questions can be classified on various continua: cognitive level based on Bloom (1956), from knowledge to evaluation; convergent to divergent; cognitive operations of concept formation, generalizing and applying, based on Taba (1971). Each of these classification systems has relevance when discussing computer-based teaching for thinking. Another method of classifying questions is input, processing, output, based on an information processing model of thinking.

Input questions involve gathering information. These questions focus on perceiving clearly, exploring systematically, labeling, perceiving temporal or spatial relationships, identifying what stays the same while other things change, or organizing or reorganizing data. Input questions in working with a computer are the questions the teacher asks to gather information about the problem.

Processing questions are those questions the teacher asks to help students make sense of the information they have gathered through input questions. Processing questions involve analyzing discrepancies, comparing and contrasting, categorizing, hypothesizing, using logical evidence to defend an opinion, building a mental image of what must be done. It is processing questions which the teacher asks more than any other type when teaching thinking skills with the computer. The questions sound like this:

- Is it good to try four new things at once? Why?
- How many possibilities are there?
- Are we positive that this is the right choice? How do we know?
- No matter what happens, will we learn anything?
- Which choice is better? Why?

FIGURE 10.6. Safari Search (Level 3)

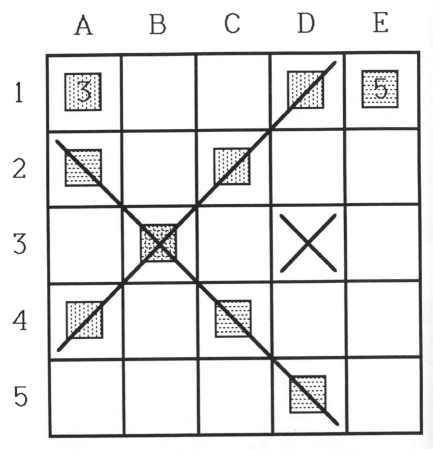

Used by permission of Sunburst Communications, Inc., Pleasantville, NY.

Output questions involve applying learnings to novel situations. Transfer of the learning about a process to a new situation is what education is intended to do for students. Such application may involve thinking through a solution rather than solving it by trial and error; formulating ideas or strategies; or checking for accuracy.

In teaching students to think using the computer, process questions become the warp of the lesson; threads of input and output questions are woven through the lesson to assist the development of process skill. Often, a three-step approach to the questioning strategy is appropriate. The question "What do you think?" establishes the student's position. Whether right or wrong, the next question needs to be, "Why do you think that?" This elicits the rationale behind the students' thinking. Follow-up questions should explore exceptions or apparent contradictions which will encourage the students to push their own thinking as far as it can go. The third question, "How did you figure it out?," asks the students to relate the steps used in arriving at the stated position.

The teacher must pursue all three steps. Whether the initial response is right or wrong is irrelevant. Once the teacher has explored the students' thinking, it is time to test the suggestion on the computer. The computer will provide feedback. Then come the questions to help students monitor their own thinking: "Why do you suppose our idea didn't work?" "What could we do differently next time?" "Why might that make a difference?" "What is different about your two responses?" "Is that difference critical? Why?"

To illustrate this three-part lesson design, what follows is a lesson for teaching Safari Search, published by Sunburst Communications.

LESSON PLANS FOR SAFARI SEARCH

Level 2—Find the Flamingo

Materials needed:
- Safari Search, Level 2, Sunburst Communications
- Large-screen monitor connected to Apple II series computer
- Post-it Notes (3M Company)

Objectives:
- The learner will formulate and test hypotheses to generate rules of the game.
- The learner will develop a strategy to arrive at an algorithm.

"A flamingo is hiding behind one of the 25 squares in the 5x5 grid. Where would you look to find him?"

The lesson is divided into three major parts:

Lesson Input:

Part 1 Using induction, the students will determine what the rules mean in the context of the program. As students choose locations on the grid, the teacher moves the X to each location and hits the return key (see Figure 10.7). The students are provided feedback in the form of three clues: "hot," "warm," and "cold." The teacher must uncover a sufficient number of locations so the students can see the correct relationships between the clues and the flamingo. At the end of the first game, all the students need to know that:

- "Hot" means "touching a side of the flamingo"
- "Warm" means "touching a corner of the flamingo"
- "Cold" means "not touching the flamingo"

FIGURE 10.7. 5x5 grid, Safari Search

	A	B	C	D	E
1	X				
2					
3					
4					
5					

Used by permission of Sunburst Communications, Inc., Pleasantville, NY.

If too few squares are opened prior to finding the flamingo during the first game, the teacher should choose "Same game" from the menu and ask students to predict the feedback behind the uncovered squares, knowing where the flamingo is hiding. After uncovering a sufficient number of squares, the students should be able to make the appropriate generalizations about the clues.

Part 2 Using hypothesis formation and testing, the students will determine the best *two* locations to choose for the first guesses (see Figure 10.8). During this portion of the instruction, the

FIGURE 10.8. Safari Search (Level 2)

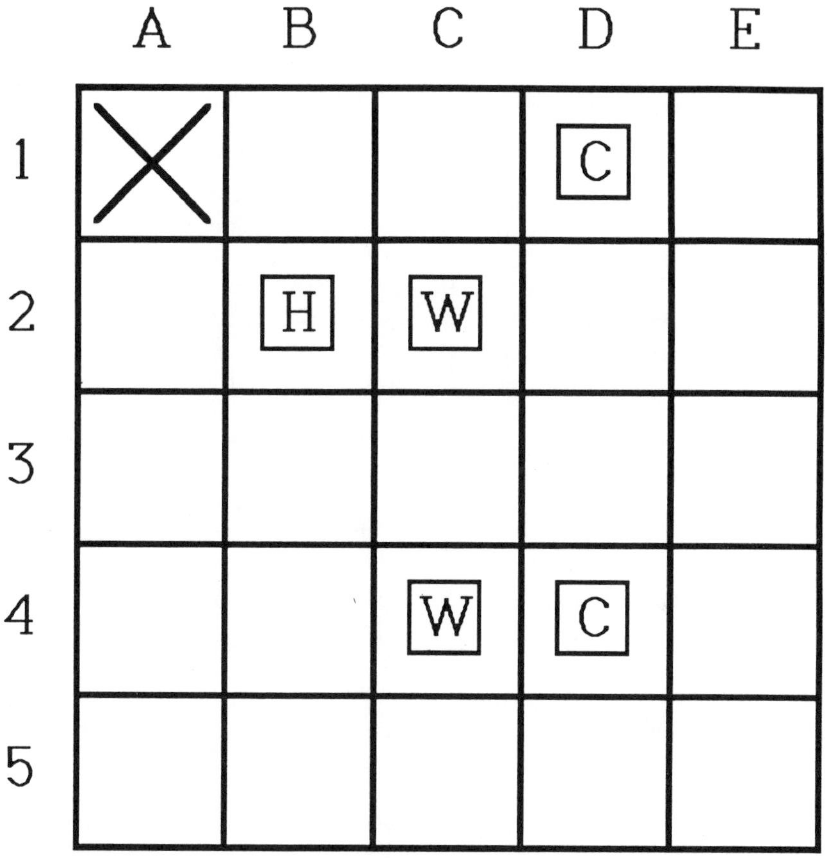

	A	B	C	D	E
1	X			C	
2		H	W		
3					
4			W	C	
5					

Used by permission of Sunburst Communications, Inc., Pleasantville, NY.

teacher uses stick-on tags to record the information on the screen. This is done instead of actually hitting the return key because the goal is to determine *what if,* not *what is.* The teacher needs to follow a strategy called "the good thinking, bad luck strategy." This means, for Safari Search, saying, "What if we guess this box and we get 'cold'?" "Cold" would seem to be the worst response; yet the next question is, "What does that tell us about where the flamingo could not be?" Some analytical thinking ensues because of the bad luck response.

In Part 2, the teacher determines what the students can deduce about the location of the flamingo. To eliminate luck the teacher tells the students they received a "cold" at each place they guessed the flamingo to be. Receiving two "colds," the fewest number of locations that can be eliminated as possible flamingo locations is six (e.g., A1 and B1). The number that can be eliminated with two "cold" responses is 17 (e.g., B2 and D4). All the numbers between 6 and 17 are possible. A very common choice of students is the middle and a corner (e.g., C3 and A1). In this instance, the number of flamingo locations eliminated is 12. By examining a middle/corner set of choices first, the teacher can constrain the thinking process to allow for a more systematic approach rather than a guess-and-check strategy. After examining C3-A1 and determining that 12 locations can be eliminated, the teacher asks students to find a 9-4 strategy, a 9-5 strategy, and then a 9-6 strategy, always keeping C3 as the first choice. Most students do not see the 9-4 at first. Almost no one sees the 9-5 without some guidance. By the time you ask them to find the 9-6 strategy, they are convinced they need to look systematically rather than haphazardly. The 9-6 is not possible with C3 as the first choice, but unless the teacher asks, students will not be convinced they have found the best strategy.

The purpose of Part 2 is to teach the students to approach systematically the process of developing a strategy. By the end of Part 2, they should have convinced themselves of the best two first guesses assuming a "cold" on the first response.

Part 3 In Part 3, the teacher tests the students' algorithm for finding the flamingo in the fewest possible moves. To eliminate luck as much as possible from the algorithm, the teacher must constrain the students' moves to disallow the guessing of a known possible flamingo location (after finding a "warm" or a "hot," there are always one, two, three, or four possible locations for the flamingo). By constraining the students' moves, the students must systematically approach the task by determining what they learn from each choice regardless of the feedback (e.g., "What do you learn if it's 'hot'? What do you learn if it's 'warm'? What do you learn if it's 'cold'?"). In this way, the students are not right or wrong. Instead they learn that by structuring a hypothesis appropriately, they will learn something worth knowing regardless of the feedback.

REFERENCES

Bloom, Benjamin S. *Taxonomy of Educational Objectives.* New York: McKay, 1956.

Costa, Art. *Developing Minds.* Alexandria, VA: Association for Supervision and Curriculum Development, 1985.

Ornstein, Allen. "Questioning: The Essence of Good Teaching." *Bulletin, National Association of Secondary School Principals* (May 1987): 71–79.

Rieber, Lloyd P. "LOGO and Its Promise: A Research Report." *Educational Technology* 27 (February, 1987): 12–16.

Taba, Hilda. *A Teacher's Handbook to Elementary Social Studies: An Inductive Approach.* Reading, MA: Addison-Wesley, 1971.

van Deusen, Robert Moon. "A Model for Teaching Thinking Skills Using One Computer, One Class, One Teacher, and Problem Solving Software." National Educational Computing Conference, Dallas, TX, June, 1988.

van Deusen, Robert M. and Jean Donham. "The Teacher's Role in Using the Computer to Teach Thinking Skills." *The Computing Teacher* 14 (January 1987): 32–34.

SOFTWARE REFERENCES

Gertrude's Puzzles. The Learning Company, Menlo Park, CA.

The Incredible Laboratory. Sunburst Communications, Pleasantville, NY.

Moptown Parade. The Learning Company, Menlo Park, CA.

Safari Search. Sunburst Communications, Pleasantville, NY.

Chapter 11
Integrating Computers into
the Mathematics Curriculum

Teachers of mathematics were among the earliest users of microcomputers within the educational setting. Many math teachers had taken classes in computer languages such as FORTRAN as a part of the requirements for a major in mathematics. For these individuals, the transition to the BASIC language utilized by most microcomputers was an easy one. In those early years, well-known figures in educational computing spoke convincingly of the need for students to learn to program; the math teacher was the obvious choice to provide such instruction. In many cases, math teachers also assumed a leadership role in selecting hardware and software and in providing training in the use of computers and programming to other teachers.

As our understanding of how computers can be used to enhance instruction has increased, and as the software available to assist such instruction has improved in quality, it has become obvious that computer programming is only one of many computer activities that can be used to support the math curriculum. The position statement issued in September 1987 by the National Council of Teachers of Mathematics (NCTM) on "The Use of Computers in the Learning and Teaching of Mathematics" states that:

> Teachers should use computers as tools to assist students with the exploration and discovery of concepts, with the transition from concrete experiences to abstract mathematical ideas, with the practice of skills, and with the process of problem solving. In mathematics education computers must be instructional aids, not the object of instruction. Similarly, computer programming activities in mathematics classes should be used to support mathematics instruction; they should not be the focus of instruction (NCTM 1987, 1-2).

Mathematics teachers are shifting their emphasis away from the use of the computer as a subject of instruction to its use as an instructional tool. In no other subject area is there so rich and varied an array of software and applications available to teachers. Indeed, the computer and the calculator have the potential to change the nature of mathematics instruction by making it possible for students to spend less time learning and practicing algorithms, which can easily be performed by the machine, and more time learning to understand mathematical concepts and how they may be used to solve problems. New national standards for mathematics education place strong emphasis on the ideas that students must become mathematical problem solvers and that they must learn to reason and communicate mathematically (NCTM 1987). These goals indicate a movement away from the traditional textbook/lecture/homework approach to math instruction toward a curriculum where students are actively involved in discussing, discovering, and using math in a variety of ways. Properly integrated and creatively used, the computer can be a powerful tool for student mathematicians.

EXPLORATION AND DISCOVERY OF CONCEPTS

In Chapter 6, we discussed Piaget's stages of children's thinking (see Figure 6.1), concluding that while primary-age children are not developmentally ready to deal with the abstractness of the computer, children aged 11 to 15 are beginning to acquire the logical thinking skills necessary to deal with abstract concepts. It is at this stage that the computer can be used to help students bridge the gap between the concrete experiences of early elementary math and the abstractness of a concept such as "variable" or the graphing of equations. Where primary students use physical manipulatives such as blocks or beans, middle school students can work in the semiconcrete to manipulate objects or angles on the computer screen. The use of the computer to aid students' understanding of mathematical concepts is by no means limited to the middle grades, however. Complex concepts encountered in high school algebra, analytical geometry, and trigonometry classes can also be explored and practiced using appropriate computer software.

Using the computer as a classroom demonstration device has proved to be highly effective for introducing math concepts. Each math classroom should be equipped with, or have ready access to, a computer attached to a large-screen T.V. monitor, or a liquid crystal display (LCD) device which enables the computer output to be viewed through an overhead projector. Using this model, the teacher can present content in algebra and geometry, and can quickly and easily modify such content on the screen as different variables are entered. The graphing of equations is one particularly useful application for this model. Where previously, the teacher or student would laboriously plot points on a coordinate plane drawn on the chalkboard, then connect the points to complete the graph of the equation, then carefully erase and begin the process again, computer programs such as Graphing Equations from CONDUIT can now accomplish the same objective in a fraction of the time. Students and teacher are free to concentrate on the concept being illustrated, rather than on the tedious drawing of lines and curves.

USING THE COMPUTER LAB

Scheduling students to use the computer lab is a second effective method for using computers in math. Students may use the lab to explore and practice concepts while the teacher circulates to provide coaching and assistance. Many teachers find that assigning students to work in pairs in the lab promotes sharing of strategies, discussion of problems, and a greater "comfort level" in working with the machines. For example, to further develop their understanding of equations introduced in the classroom demonstration, students might be scheduled to use the highly acclaimed "Green Globs" portion of Graphing Equations in the computer lab (see Figure 11.1). In "Green

FIGURE 11.1. Demonstrating the Use of "Green Globs" to Students

Used by permission of the software developer, CONDUIT, Iowa City, IA.

Globs," students are provided with an axis on which 13 green dots are scattered randomly. Students type in an equation for a graph that will intersect as many as possible of the points represented by the "green globs"; when the globs are hit, they explode. If a student's graph fails to hit the points expected, feedback is given to help the student make the needed corrections. "Green Globs" provides students with an opportunity to apply what they have learned about graphs; if students are assigned to work in pairs on the program, they also become involved in sharing and verbalizing their knowledge. The program includes both a novice and an expert level and can be used by students in classes from beginning algebra through trigonometry (Dugdale 1984).

LOGO is a software tool that can be used to help students discover and explore concepts in geometry. Developed at M.I.T. in the late 1960s by a group headed by Seymour Papert, LOGO is a programming language that utilizes simple commands such as FORWARD, RIGHT, or LEFT to instruct a small triangle, usually called the "turtle," to move around on the computer screen. LOGO has been widely heralded as a means of developing thinking skills; such use is discussed in Chapter 10.

Students usually begin to explore concepts in geometry through the use of concrete experiences such as folding paper into geometric shapes or manipulating mirrors to discover relationships between lines and angles. LOGO, or "turtle geometry," is a logical next step in the students' understanding of the concepts of plane geometry, forming a bridge between these early concrete experiences and the abstractions of theorems and proofs (Martin and Bearden 1985). For example, students might be asked to write a LOGO program or procedure to draw a triangle. In order to do this, they must develop a definition of what makes a triangle, express that definition in the language of LOGO by writing the procedure, and then test their understanding by running the program. As students develop procedures for constructing angles, polygons, and other figures, they become active participants in learning the concepts of geometry. Such learning does not simply occur spontaneously; it must be closely guided by the teacher through the design of the LOGO lessons to be completed by the student. And, as in any lab situation, the teacher must be constantly available to intervene with directed questions when students are having difficulty, and to check that students make the correct connections between their LOGO activities and the mathematical concepts being addressed (Battista 1987).

Using a series of programs called the Geometric Supposers, students can also create various geometric figures on the computer screen and then make conjectures about the shapes and the rules of geometry by bisecting the shapes or manipulating them in other ways. Using these programs involves students in a process that resembles the scientific method as they set up a problem, make conjectures about that problem, gather and analyze data related to their conjectures, and then write proofs for the conjectures. This software is appropriate for students just beginning to study geometry (Geometric Presupposer) up through high school (see Figure 11.2). With careful guidance by the teacher, both LOGO and the Supposers actively involve students in discussing and practicing geometry rather than simply listening to someone lecture about it (Yerushalmy and Houde 1986).

FIGURE 11.2. Exploring the Properties of Quadrilaterals, Using the Geometric Presupposer from Sunburst

Used by permission of Sunburst Communications, Inc., Pleasantville, NY.

PRACTICING SKILLS

Much of the early software developed for math was of the drill-and-practice or "drill-and-kill" variety. Students were to sit at the keyboard and type in answers to randomly selected problems designed to increase their speed and accuracy in the various arithmetic procedures. Often they would be rewarded for correct answers by having an alien spaceship fall out of the sky, or in some other way, usually unrelated to the objective of the program. While such programs may be motivational, they fail to take advantage of the real power of the computer, and, in the words of Glenn Fisher, simply enable us to do many of the "worst things faster" (O'Brien 1986, 41). Indeed, some researchers have found no significant difference in the outcome of practicing math facts on the computer and using the more traditional flash card method (Fuson and Brinko 1986). Given the relative cost of the two methods, the use of flash cards would seem to make the best sense. However, in some situations where students are learning complex new skills, well-designed software can be an appropriate method of providing practice. For example, the almost universal use of calculators today makes the skill of estimating the results of arithmetic computations a crucial one. Students must be able to judge whether the results appearing on the calculator are of the proper magnitude—in other words, if they are in the ballpark. The use of a program such as Power Drill to provide practice in estimation represents an improvement over other types of drill because it can respond to students' incorrect answers by providing clues and strategies for improving. This could not be done otherwise unless a teacher was working one to one with the student. Drill-and-practice software is appropriate when it provides us with a better way of reinforcing skills than was possible in the past.

Many textbook publishers are now developing software to accompany textbook lessons. This is a trend that bears careful watching. Many educators, including the influential California Superintendent of Public Instruction, William Honig, have decried the relatively poor quality of most textbooks. Since current textbook series focus heavily on repetition and review, it is likely that software designed to accompany textbooks would be primarily of the drill and practice variety. A better approach is for teachers to identify software that is tied to the goals of their curriculum. Figure 11.3 illustrates how commercially available software can be used to provide students with the opportunity to practice and develop the skills covered in several units of a pre-algrebra class, typically taught in junior high school. In each case, the computer is used to clarify a concept or practice a new skill; it can be used as a classroom demonstration device or in a lab setting to provide for individual practice in developing a concept. In either mode, the teacher must make clear the objectives of the program and carefully model its use for students. If using the computer lab, the teacher must circulate among the students, serving as coach, asking appropriate questions and checking for on-task behavior and understanding.

PROBLEM SOLVING

A basic goal of teaching mathematics is to enable students to solve real-life problems. New national standards for mathematics place heavy emphasis on the teaching of problem solving. The use of the computer and various commercially available software to teach problem-solving skills such as hypothesizing, organizing data, drawing inferences, using inductive and deductive reasoning, and comparing and contrasting is described in detail in Chapter 10. The model presented there em-

FIGURE 11.3. A Model for Integrating Computers into the Pre-Algebra Class

Unit	Software	Objective
Number Properties and Patterns	*The King's Rule* Sunburst, 1984.	Discover patterns and sequences in problems
Number Theory	*Number Stumper* Houghton Mifflin Mathematics Activities Courseware, 1984.	Illustrates relationships involving factors and multiples
Estimation	*Power Drill* Sunburst, 1986.	Provides practice in estimating
Integers and Number Sentences	*Solving Equations and Inequalities* Sunburst, 1987.	Solving of equations is modeled with a balance
Geometric Figures	LOGO Terrapin, 1982.	Allows student to discover concepts in plane geometry
Rational Numbers and Number Sentences	*Eckses and Ohzs* Houghton Mifflin Mathematics Activities Courseware, 1984.	Develops skill in solving equations and inverse operations
Using Geometry	*Geometric Presupposer* Sunburst, 1986.	Students explore and form generalizations about shapes and relationships
Percent with Applications	*Appleworks* (or other spreadsheet) Apple Computer, Inc., 1986.	Student can manipulate percents to explore concept
Geometric Transformations	*The Right Turn* Sunburst, 1985.	Develops visual thinking skills such as rotation, flipping, and translations
Probability and Statistics	*MECC Graph* MECC, 1985.	Helps students interpret through graphic representation
Functions and Graphs	*Interpreting Graphs* Conduit, 1982.	Helps students understand relationships shown by graphs.

phasizes separating the process from subject-area content, so that student attention becomes focused on his or her own thinking. This method is highly appropriate for mathematics at all levels.

Problem solving can also be taught within the content of mathematics to show the relationship between mathematics and real-life applications. Recent studies indicate that while students may have attained a mastery of an operation such as multiplying whole numbers, they often have little idea of when to use this knowledge. Such studies call for a greater emphasis on using math to solve realistic problems rather than solely on learning and practicing procedures (Driscoll 1988). Students must know "why" and "when" in addition to knowing "how."

The use of databases and spreadsheets in mathematics provides an opportunity for students to participate in realistic problem solving activities within the school setting. An activity was described in Chapter 8 in which a database was constructed from student responses to a series of questions such as "What is your favorite subject?" "Are you right- or left-handed?" "How many hours each week do you spend watching television?" "What is your grade point average?" Students were taught about the concepts of sorting and searching using Boolean operators and then searched the database to answer a series of questions. Such an activity could easily be used in the math classroom, where students might be asked such questions as "What percentage of eighth grade students are left-handed?" "Is there a relationship between the dominant hand and students' favorite subjects?" and "Do students with higher grade point averages watch less T.V. than those with lower G.P.A.s?" In completing such an activity, students are asked to develop a strategy for solving each problem, make conjectures, and apply knowledge of math procedures in order to answer the questions.

Spreadsheets can be used to demonstrate a variety of real-world problems. For example, high school students often develop a strong interest in owning automobiles. A spreadsheet might be used to help students understand various relationships between factors such as the original cost of the car, the size of the down payment, the interest rate charged for a loan, and the term of the loan. Once the student has determined the proper formulas to use within the spreadsheet, he or she can use this tool to ask "what if" questions. Information entered into a spreadsheet can also be printed out in the form of a pie chart or graph, thus enabling the student to see a visual representation of comparative interest rates or gas mileage. By manipulating information in this way, students can readily see the value of using the spreadsheet as a decision-making tool. Arganbright (1984) has suggested a number of applications of the spreadsheet in mathematics, including solving word problems in algebra, trigonometry, and calculus; modeling rates of growth; and executing algorithms.

Statistics has become an increasingly important area of study in our information-rich world; students begin to study probability and statistics as early as seventh grade. A major function of statistics is to reduce large amounts of data to understandable information which can be used to make decisions. Often in studying statistics, student effort becomes concentrated so heavily on the complicated calculations required to determine standard deviations or correlation coefficients that the concept of interpreting information is lost. A computer spreadsheet is ideally suited to perform the iterative computations required to produce descriptive and inferential measures in statistics.

Students can then concentrate their efforts on understanding the concepts and their application.

Spreadsheets can be used with students when they are introduced to the concept of variables. Spreadsheets and databases have important applications in mathematics; students must understand when it is appropriate to use these tools for problem solving.

PROGRAMMING

Within the math curriculum, the NCTM (1987) recommends that programming activities be used to support mathematics instruction, but not be the focus of instruction. Programming classes, often taught by the math department, continue to be offered as elective classes for students with a strong interest in the subject. This is certainly appropriate as long as sufficient equipment is available to support the needs of the required curriculum as well. Programming can also be used as one method of allowing students to experience real-world problem solving. In constructing a procedure, or program, for execution by a computer, students must follow a problem-solving model: defining the problem, determining the steps to be followed to solve the problem, testing the solution, and revising the program as necessary to achieve the desired result. This type of organized thinking process is fundamental to all problem solving. Encountering programming at some point in the math curriculum fulfils the computer literacy goal of making students aware of how a computer functions in following directions, and can make the abilities and limitations of the computer clearer to students. Students should realize that a computer can only follow the instructions that it is given in the way they are given; "garbage in, garbage out" is the phrase usually used to illustrate the results of a faulty program. While it is useful for all students to understand the concept of programming and how it is used to give instructions to the computer, mastery of programming should not be required for all students.

SUMMARY

Current research in math education points to a need to move away from the heavy emphasis on learning and practicing procedures to an emphasis on teaching students how to apply mathematical thinking to real-life problem solving situations. Both the computer and the calculator can serve as tools to facilitate that goal since both are well-suited to performing routine, repetitive procedures, freeing students to be involved in creative thinking and problem solving. Computers should be integrated into mathematics instruction in ways that make it possible for students to grasp concepts more quickly, and for students to spend less time learning math and more time doing math.

APPLYING MATH CONCEPTS WITH THE FACTORY

The following lesson serves as a model of how the computer can be used to fulfill a number of goals within the math curriculum. This sample lesson, appropriate for students in grades 8 through 11, illustrates how the computer can be integrated into the mathematics curriculum to enable students to apply math skills and concepts to realistic situations. In this lesson, students use the software package The Factory to design products in the most cost-effective manner possible. In The Factory, punching and "striping" machines are manipulated on the computer screen to produce a variety of products. For example, a product might be punched with two holes, and then rotated 90 degrees and striped horizontally to produce the product shown in Figure 11.4. Given a product with a specific design, students must work backward, a valuable problem-solving skill, to determine the most efficient means of producing a product.

After they become proficient users of The Factory, students are given a $25,000 budget to establish a manufacturing operation. They must decide whether to buy or rent a building, how much equipment to purchase, and what wages to pay employees based upon projected production costs and profits per unit. At this stage in the lesson, students use a spreadsheet to assist in their decision making. Throughout this activity, students work together in cooperative learning groups, which further simulates real-world problem solving. This unit would also be appropriate for an interdisciplinary teaching activity with a social studies department or for use in an economics class (St. John 1988).

Lesson Plans: Building a Factory

Materials needed:

- The Factory computer software
- A spreadsheet program such as Appleworks
- One microcomputer per group of four students
- Assorted informational and decision-making worksheets prepared by the instructor

Objectives:

1. The learner will use the program The Factory to develop visual discrimination, spatial perception, and logic skills.
2. The learner will apply his or her mathematical knowledge in solving a series of problems.

FIGURE 11.4. The Factory—Using Machines that Stripe, Rotate, and Punch to Build Products

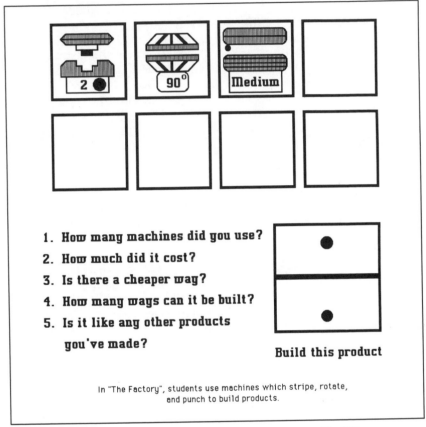

1. Hom mang machines did gou use?
2. Hom much did it cost?
3. Is there a cheaper mag?
4. Hom mang mags can it be built?
5. Is it like ang other products gou've made?

Build this product

In "The Factory", students use machines which stripe, rotate, and punch to build products.

Used by permission of Sunburst Communications, Inc., Pleasantville, NY.

3. The learner will use a spreadsheet to organize and compare numerical data.
4. The learner will analyze and evaluate alternatives in constructing a simulated manufacturing operation.
5. The learners will work in groups, experiencing a team approach to problem solving.

Lesson Input:

Discuss the general process of manufacturing eliciting as much student input as possible. Cover concepts such as raw materials, steps in manufacture, packaging and distribution of the product, and profit and loss.

Modeling:

The instructor will model the use of The Factory using the classroom demonstration method.

The instructor will assign groups and roles and model how each group member is expected to function.

The instructor will demonstrate the use of the decision-making worksheets.

The instructor will demonstrate the use of the spreadsheet.

Guided Practice:

Students will work in their groups in the computer lab to practice use of The Factory and to determine the cheapest way to make products.

Students will work in groups to make decisions relative to the establishment of their factory.

Students will use the spreadsheet to manipulate data such as costs of raw materials, wages, overhead costs, and price of equipment to arrive at the most efficient means of filling orders for products.

During the time students are working in groups, the instructor will be circulating to ask guiding questions, to facilitate group processes, and to check for understanding.

Summary:

At the end of each day, one group member will be selected to report his or her group's progress and problems to the rest of the class. Discussion will be guided by the instructor to increase students' awareness of difficulties and decisions involved in a manufacturing operation.

REFERENCES

Arganbright, Deane E. "Mathematical Applications of an Electronic Spreadsheet." *Computers in Mathematics Education: NCTM 1984 Yearbook.* Reston, VA: NCTM, 1984.

Battista, Michael T. "MATHSTUFF Logo Procedures: Bridging the Gap between Logo and School Geometry." *Arithmetic Teacher* 33 (September, 1987): 7–10.

Driscoll, Mark. "Transforming the 'Underachieving' Math Curriculum." *ASCD Curriculum Update* (January, 1988): 1–7.

Dugdale, Sharon. "Green Globs: A Microcomputer Application for Graphing of Equations." *Mathematics Teacher* 75 (March, 1982): 208–14.

Fuson, K. C. and K. T. Brinko. "The Comparative Effectiveness of Microcomputers and Flash Cards in the Drill and Practice of Basic Mathematics Facts." *Journal of Research in Mathematics Education* 16 (September, 1985): 225–32.

Martin, Kathleen and Bearden, Donna. *Mathematics and Logo: A Turtle Trip through Geometry.* Reston, VA: Reston Publishing Co., Inc., 1985.

National Council of Teachers of Mathematics. "The Use of Computers in the Learning and Teaching of Mathematics." Reston, VA: NCTM, 1987, 1–2.

O'Brien, Tom. "Turning Mysteries Into Problems: Software for Developing Thinking Skills." *The Computing Teacher* 13 (March, 1986): 39–43.

St. John, Dennis. "Using *The Factory* to Start a Business." NCTM Regional Conference; St. Louis, MO, October, 1988.

Yerushalmy, Michael and Richard A. Houde. "The Geometric Supposer: Promoting Thinking and Learning." *Mathematics Teacher* 79 (September, 1986): 418–22.

SOFTWARE REFERENCES

Appleworks. Apple Computer, Inc., Cupertino, CA.

The Factory. Sunburst Communications, Pleasantville, NY.

Geometric Presupposers. Sunburst Communications, Pleasantville, NY.

Geometric Supposers. Sunburst Communications, Pleasantville, NY.

Graphing Equations. CONDUIT, Iowa City, IA.

LOGO. Terrapin, Inc., Cambridge, MA.

Power Drill. Sunburst Communications, Pleasantville, NY.

Chapter 12
Using Computers in Social Studies

In addition to developing in students a sound base of knowledge about our world and its history, the social studies curriculum includes the goals of developing critical thinking and helping students to acquire decision-making skills, the ability to locate and interpret information, and the understandings and attitudes necessary for citizenship. To attain these objectives, social studies teachers employ a variety of methodologies including small- and large-group work, simulations, and role playing, and a variety of media such as film, filmstrips and video. The computer can also be used as a tool in fulfilling the goals of the social studies program.

LARGE-GROUP PRESENTATIONS

The lecture is perhaps the most common teaching method employed in social studies. The use of the computer as a classroom demonstration device can enhance the presentation of information to students. Connected to a large-screen monitor or overhead display device, the computer can be used to visually illustrate difficult concepts. Suppose, for example, that an instructor was presenting information on population growth. A goal of the lecture might be to make students aware of the effects of different fertility and mortality rates on a country's population over time. Using a program called Demo-graphics, the teacher can manipulate these rates; the computer will generate graphs which illustrate the changes brought about by differing combinations (see Figure 12.1). The teacher could further use the computer to improve the content of the presentation by posing to students a series of "what if" questions: "If the life expectancy of its people increases by two years, what will the population of Mexico be in the year 2000?" "What if the infant mortality rate declines?" "What if the fertility rate decreases?" The computer can quickly calculate and illustrate the answers to these questions. This

FIGURE 12.1. A Demonstration of Demo-graphics, allowing the Teacher to Demonstrate Concepts Related to Population Growth

Used by permission of the software developer, CONDUIT, Iowa City, IA.

program is suitable for secondary school classes in sociology, world affairs, and area studies.

A program called Annam provides another example of whole-class use of the computer. In this program, the student is asked to play the role of the ruler of a hypothetical Asian kingdom which is being threatened by a neighboring country. Decisions must be made about such problems as handling protestors and accepting aid from other countries. The typical use would be for students to work through the program alone or with a partner to amass as many points as possible. In this context, the program becomes little more than another "educational" game. Instead, by using the program in a large-group format, the teacher can guide students to be more careful in their decision making by considering various alternatives and their consequences. At one point in the program, for example, the threat to the country is so severe that the ruler is forced to draft 10,000 soldiers into the army. However, it is rice planting season, and if 10,000 men are drafted, the effect on the crops will be severe. The class must discuss the pros and cons of each action before proceeding. This type of exercise in decision making helps students 'understand the principle of cause and effect and some of the problems political leaders face, and could be used to enhance a lecture in political science, world affairs, or government.

Another example of one creative teacher's approach to using the computer in a large-group setting involves the use of the popular program Where in the World Is Carmen Sandiego? from Broderbund. This program, in which the player travels around the world pursuing various criminals, is great fun and has been widely purchased as a home entertainment program for families. However, along with its sequels, Where in the U.S.A. Is Carmen Sandiego? and Where in Europe Is Carmen Sandiego?, the program can also teach geographical concepts and locations and the use of specific reference books such as atlases, almanacs, and geographical dictionaries. Again, using the large-group format, the teacher introduces the reference sources and explains their use. The teacher controls the flow of the game on the computer while students work with a partner to decide what the next move should be. For example, if a clue were given that the criminal requested information on the Rappahannock River, students would search their geographical dictionaries or atlases to discover where that river is located. Students also gain practice in taking notes while using this program since they must keep records on the criminal's characteristics so that the criminal can be identified prior to arrest. Carmen Sandiego might be used as a team-teaching activity involving the social studies teacher and the library media specialist at the middle school level (Myers 1988).

In examining software, social studies teachers should not overlook the potential for the computer to be used for large-group presentations. Such use can involve students more actively in the learning process and provide a vehicle for developing thinking and decision-making skills.

SIMULATIONS

Simulations have long been used in social studies classrooms to afford students an opportunity to replicate real-world events. Computerized simulations have added a new dimension to this teaching method, as they allow the student to participate in activities which would otherwise be too costly, dangerous, or simply impractical. Simulations take advantage of one of the powerful features of the computer—its ability to be interactive. When the student makes a choice or decision within a simulation, the computer generates a response based upon that choice. In a well-designed simulation, the response closely approximates what might happen in real life. Simulations require the student to build a mental model of a process or event. He or she can then see how that process or event is altered by making different choices (Alessi and Trollip 1985).

An excellent way for students to use computer simulations is by assigning them to work in cooperative learning groups (see Figure 12.2). Based upon the work of Roger Johnson and David Johnson (1985) of the University of Minnesota, cooperative learning has received increasing attention recently for its potential to allow students to learn from each other and to learn group process skills. The key to cooperative learning is "positive interdependence," students working together toward mutual goals in such a way that the labor is shared and members of the group must depend upon each other. Such skills as leadership, conflict resolution, and decision making are taught and practiced in a cooperative learning situation.

FIGURE 12.2. Cooperative Learning at the Computer

The Search series of programs produced by Tom Snyder for McGraw-Hill provides a vehicle for computer simulation to be done in cooperative learning groups. In Archeology Search students explore the location of a seventeenth-century settlement. The goal is for students to find out as much as they can about the site and its inhabitants. In the process of using the program, students experience the methods of research, mapping, recording and decision making used by archaeologists. To use the program, students are divided into teams, or cooperative learning groups. Each member of the group has specific responsibilities for which she or he is accountable: one is chosen as the team leader, one the recorder, one the mapper, one the person who does the actual typing into the computer. The groups take turns at the computer; thus, two or three computers will be sufficient for an entire class. During their turn at the computer, the team will enter coordinates at which they want to "dig." The computer will respond by indicating if anything was found at that location, and if so, what. When not at the computer, students must log and map their findings, and plan what their strategy will be when their turn comes again. Readings provide some clues about where digging should be done. In using this simulation, students learn to work together to solve problems through group consensus. The teacher makes evaluations on the basis of the performance of each group.

There are many examples of computer simulations for social studies. Another Tom Snyder production, The Other Side, involves students in balancing the economic needs of two opposing nations in order to preserve world peace. This is a complex simulation suitable for use in a high school economics or political science class. It can also be used by participants from different schools via modem. New computer simulations and role-playing programs are entering the market daily. Such programs provide an opportunity for students to apply their background in social studies to decision making in realistic situations.

Two cautions apply to the use of computer simulations. First, the teacher must carefully structure the simulation and relate it clearly to classroom goals. Most simulations require some research and preparation so that the students understand the context of the situation. Teachers must insist that students keep careful records of events and decisions which occur within the simulation. Unless the teacher is actively involved in preparing students and monitoring progress during the simulation, it becomes little more than a game for the students. The MECC program Oregon Trail provides one example of how a good program can be badly misused. As one of the earliest examples of a microcomputer-based simulation, it was purchased by many schools. Students were allowed to "play" Oregon Trail without any of the research or journal-keeping activities recommended by its authors, with the result that it became little more than a hunting game. By the time most students reached the point where they studied the westward movement in social studies, they had already used Oregon Trail so much that it had lost its usefulness as a teaching tool. The teacher must plan simulation lessons as carefully and thoughtfully as any other instructional activity. The second caution is that to do a simulation properly requires a significant amount of time. The Archeology Search simulation described above requires a minimum of five class periods. Teachers must be sure that the learning outcomes justify this time commitment.

APPLICATIONS SOFTWARE IN SOCIAL STUDIES

In addition to serving the social studies curriculum as an interactive teaching tool assisting the teacher in the delivery of content, computer technology can also assist the student in processing the presented information. The computer is an effective information delivery and management device. The social studies curriculum offers numerous opportunities for the incorporation of "applications" software—programs designed for information manipulation, management, and presentation. Word processing programs, database management systems, spreadsheet systems, and graphing programs all have a place in social studies.

Word Processing

The opportunities for word processing are apparent. Students in social studies are often required to do writing, from formal research papers to short biographical sketches on prominent historical figures. Many schools have made a commitment to the concept of "writing across the curriculum," where classroom teachers from many curricular areas are encouraged not only to have their students write, but also to provide feedback on that writing. It is hoped that students will become better writers and that they will better perceive the need for writing skills. Writing is no longer something done only in English/language arts classes.

The advantages of using word processing have been described in an earlier chapter. If given the opportunity, most students will use word processing for many of their writing assignments in any class. To encourage and facilitate students' use of word processing, social studies teachers should try to schedule the use of the computer lab during writing assignments so that the computers are more readily available to the students. For example, many social studies teachers will assign a report and bring the class to the library media center for several days, allowing some in-class time to do research. Along with reserving space in the media center, the teacher should make arrangements to allow students to work in the computer lab as they finish researching and begin to write.

One example of a teacher encouraging the creative use of word processing capabilities involves a junior high history teacher whose students produce "colonial newspapers" each year. Working in small groups, the students must research various aspects of American colonial life and write appropriate newspaper articles. They research and compose such items as feature articles, advice columns, political cartoons, obituaries, recipes, and classified ads as well as the news of the day, all accurate as to time and setting. Some students use The Newsroom, a word processing program designed specifically to produce newspapers, allowing for columns, various text fonts, and graphics. Other students choose to use the standard word processing program they are comfortable with, simply setting the left and right margins so that the text prints in narrow columns. They use The Print Shop to produce special headlines and graphics. Finally, they manually paste up their articles into columns and add the graphics. The finished pages are photocopied for a polished look.

Databases

The use of database management programs in social studies is increasing rapidly. As described in Chapter 9, one of the benefits of teaching with a database is that it can serve as a vehicle for organizing and presenting content information for analysis. Classroom teachers are realizing the potential that database use has in developing higher order thinking skills and in presenting information for the students to work with. To use databases, students must learn to formulate the sort routines and searching strategies necessary to address the information need a particular problem poses. Databases allow students to integrate their learning of subject area content with new information processing skills. Recently, numerous database programs have been developed in the social studies field, ranging from data files contained on a simple database system to richly detailed files designed to be used on the more powerful standard database management systems such as PFS: File or Appleworks.

An appropriate progression of database skill calls for students to first learn to use and manipulate a database created by someone else. In this type of activity, the student is confronted with various questions or problems and must analyze the information in the database by performing searches of the data to determine the solution to the problem. The second stage of database skill involves the student in gathering the data to be entered into an already established database template before performing manipulations of the data. In the final stage of database skill the student designs the database file itself, determining the type of data needed to solve the problem at hand, then setting up the fields and layout of record. The student gathers and enters the data, and accesses the data to assimilate the needed information.

An example of the first stage of database use involves an immigration unit in a junior high history class where an Appleworks database, Immigrant, the Irish Experience, is used with the students. The purpose of the database activity is to allow the students to begin to perceive the severe conditions which confronted the Irish immigrants arriving in Boston in the mid 1800s. The database contains facts about numerous immigrants, the type of jobs and wages available, and the type and cost of housing, transportation, food, and clothing. Students develop a survival plan for an immigrant family, requiring that they sort through much of the database to examine the possibilities and make logical decisions based on the data.

In another activity students add data to a locally created global statistics database. Pairs of students are assigned a country for which they must locate such information as birth and death rates, infant mortality rate, literacy rate, energy consumption, caloric intake, chief resources, imports, and exports. After the data are entered into the database, the students are given problems requiring them to sort and search the information in the data file in several ways to see patterns, determine correlations, make predictions, and draw conclusions about the significance of various demographic factors.

Polls and Politics is a program which can be used to introduce students to political polls, and teach them how polls have developed, and how they have become a vital, integral component of the American political system. The program also demonstrates the influence of the computer in the development of more sophisticated polling techniques. The lessons begin with a discussion of how political polls are used in elections, how they can be analyzed and evaluated, and what effect the polls can have on campaigns and election results. Data that the students collect from a survey can be entered into the computer program for analysis, computation, and printing of the results to model how the computer is actually used in political elections. Once students understand how the polls operate, how to construct a valid survey instrument, and how to analyze poll results, the program can be used as a data management tool in other student projects involving survey analysis or polls. Students could plan and conduct surveys of the demographics of the school or public opinion on a recent event using the Polls and Politics program as data manager.

The third stage of using a database involves students in designing their own database template to solve a particular problem or organize and access needed information. Student government often operates as a part of the social studies program. Officers of the Student Council might set up a database to keep records on the various members of the council such as which homeroom they represent, their addresses and phone numbers, and their special strengths and interests. The database could then be searched for students interested in working on a dance committee or those who could design posters for an upcoming event.

A database management program extends the capacity to access, probe and analyze information. A recent article on the content of the social studies curriculum speaks to the need for students to learn to "use data to make meaning" and to "think using different logical patterns and perspectives" (Bragaw and Hartoonian 1988, 12). Because information can be sorted and selectively examined, a database allows students to look at information through different windows, giving them different perspectives upon which to make decisions or draw conclusions.

Spreadsheets

A third type of application software which is relevant for some social studies classrooms is a spreadsheet program. Because of its complex computational capabilities, a spreadsheet can be used to "track" various numerical phenomena such as population, immigration patterns, worldwide food production, or business-related production costs.

A common activity in the high school economics class involves the study of the stock market; students are often required to follow the performance of a particular stock over a period of several months. A spreadsheet program allows the student to use the computer to analyze the fluctuations of a particular stock and determine if it is a good investment over time. The activity might be set up as follows. Each student is "given" the sum of $1,000 to invest in the stock market for a period of three months. Students are required to research stocks of interest and decide upon two companies in which to invest. Students use a spreadsheet to track the performance of the stocks on a weekly basis during the course of the activity. At the end of three months, students compute the value of their stocks, including the dividend issued by the companies. Figure 12.3 illustrates how this simulation activity might be set up on a spreadsheet. An added

FIGURE 12.3. A Spreadsheet Program Used to Track the Performance of Stocks and Graph the Results

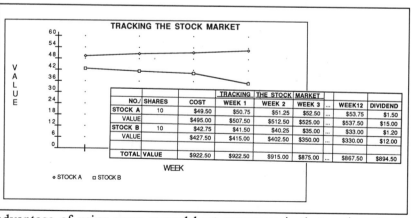

TRACKING THE STOCK MARKET

	NO./ SHARES	COST	TRACKING THE STOCK MARKET WEEK 1	WEEK 2	WEEK 3	...	WEEK12	DIVIDEND
STOCK A	10	$49.50	$50.75	$51.25	$52.50	...	$53.75	$1.50
VALUE		$495.00	$507.50	$512.50	$525.00	...	$537.50	$15.00
STOCK B	10	$42.75	$41.50	$40.25	$35.00	...	$33.00	$1.20
VALUE		$427.50	$415.00	$402.50	$350.00	...	$330.00	$12.00
TOTAL VALUE		$922.50	$922.50	$915.00	$875.00	...	$867.50	$894.50

⬦ STOCK A ▫ STOCK B

advantage of using some spreadsheet programs is that various types of graphs can be generated to visually illustrate the information given.

Graphing Software

Another computer application useful in social studies is a graphing program which produces a visual representation based on the numerical data entered by the user. This can be an effective teacher utility, providing a simple means for generating statistics in graph form to help students interpret information visually when raw numbers alone are difficult to comprehend. A graphing program is also a valuable tool for students when they are attempting to report results of their research. A graphing utility program such as the simple-to-use MECC Graph quickly generates either a bar graph, a line graph or a pie graph. Such a program might be used in combination with a database or spreadsheet to help bring meaning to a large amount of information.

SOCIAL ISSUES RELATED TO COMPUTERS

We have recommended that computer literacy activities be integrated into the existing curriculum. If a student is to be considered computer literate upon graduation from high school, it is essential that she or he be knowledgeable about the social and ethical issues involved in computer use. Social studies is the logical place to explore these issues, which might be divided into three elements: (1) computer crime, (2) the right to privacy, and (3) the impact of technology on future life.

Computer crime is primarily a young person's crime. At the simplest level, it occurs when students make copies of software belonging to their friends. At its most devious, it involves hackers who use their programming expertise to sabotage the huge, expensive databases maintained by government and the military. In spite of increasingly sophisticated copy protection and security systems, it seems that programmers may never be able to develop a system that some other programmer won't be able to break into. Of course, the costs of developing such security systems must be passed on to the consumer or taxpayer. The problem of students making illegal copies of disks has been around as long as the microcomputer has been in the schools. This problem is not the sole responsibility of the social studies program; indeed, it must be discussed and confronted in all areas where computers are used from the earliest ages. One of the most powerful of teaching tools is the modeling of appropriate behavior; schools must insist that staff as well as students abide by copyright laws. Computer-assisted plagiarism may also become a problem as more schools and individuals have access to online databases. Discussion of these legal and ethical issues should take place in social studies as students deal with the entire area of technology and its effects on our lives.

A second key area for discussion in social studies is the question of the computer and its effect on privacy. An appropriate time to begin to explore the issue of privacy is when students start to study databases. For example, as a beginning database activity, we have made use of a collection of student data which include each individual's grade point average. The database does not give names. Even so, some students are reluctant to enter their G.P.A.s. This situation provides an excellent opportunity to explore the question of individual privacy. Students can brainstorm a list of all of the databases that contain personal information on them or their family. Medical records, tax records, credit union ratings, bank records, and school records are well-known examples. Students can be asked to discuss who should have access to this information and how it should be safeguarded. They should also understand that there is a legitimate need to know in many cases. For example, someone who applies for a credit card must expect that the company to which he or she applies will request a financial history. As the First Amendment is discussed in history and government classes, the issues of freedom of information and the right to privacy as they relate to the use of computers should be addressed.

Much has been written about the effect of technology on life in the future. Alvin Toffler (1970) wrote about a phenomenon he labeled "future shock," the feeling that things are changing too fast and that individuals are not prepared for the future in which they find themselves. John Naisbitt (1982) coined the phrase "high tech/high touch" to describe our reaction to increased use of technology: As new technologies enter our lives we respond with a need for more personal contact and control. One example is the fact that at the same time robots have been introduced to factory situations on a large scale, quality circle groups have developed. Naisbitt uses this same argument to counter the notion of the "electronic cottage," where people work at a home computer linked by modem to the workplace. People want to go to the office, he says, and they want to be with other people. Another aspect of future life with obvious implications for social studies is the likelihood that students will live and work in a world economy. They will communicate, either face to face or electronically, with people from a variety of cultures.

There are several other issues to be addressed as students study the impact of technology on human life. Students should have an understanding of what computers can and cannot do. Artificial intelligence and the use of expert systems for decision making in the social sciences and other areas should be discussed. Students should be aware of what the information age is, of how they can access information for their own uses. Economics classes will surely discuss the cashless society and the implications that has for personal finances. Regardless of one's vision of the future, it is obvious that technology will change the way we work. Students must be prepared for the frequent job retraining that will occur during their careers. The social studies curriculum should contain a strand where these issues are studied and discussed thoroughly, so that students graduating from high school possess a confident understanding of the future they are stepping into.

SUMMARY

Computers can enhance the social studies curriculum in many ways. Demonstration and simulation programs can be used to improve upon existing teaching methods. The use of applications software, particularly database programs, provides students with a powerful tool for managing the large amounts of information encountered in the social studies. The ethical use of computers and the effect technology will have on life in the future are important areas for consideration within the social studies curriculum.

A LESSON IN COMPUTER ETHICS

The following social studies lesson introduces to the student ethical issues related to the use of software.

Materials Needed:
- Overhead projector
- Newspaper clipping involving the prosecution of hackers
- Cards with written scenarios regarding computer ethics; examples include disk piracy, database tampering, theft of information from online databases, plagiarism from online databases.

Objectives:
1. The learner will explore his or her attitudes about ethical uses of computers.
2. The learner will explain and defend his or her opinions about computer ethics issues.
3. The learner will analyze the opinions of others on computer ethics issues.
4. The learner will write a statement of his or her beliefs about each of the areas discussed.

Lesson Input:
The instructor will present information on the ethical issues involving computer use. Points to be covered include:

1. Copyright law and the reasons for its existence.

2. Information about huge databases maintained by government and business, the ways databases have been tampered with by hackers, and the results of such tampering.
3. The First Amendment and its implications for both individual privacy and freedom of information.

Modeling:
The instructor will model with the class the discussion of one of the scenarios involving computer ethics. The group should come up with arguments on both sides of the question.
SAMPLE SCENARIO:
Bill has just purchased a copy of the computer video game Star Trackers. Bill and his friend Amy play the game for several hours on Saturday. Amy enjoys the game and asks Bill to make her a copy. What would you do if you were Bill?

Arguments for making the copy:
Bill paid for the game; he can share it if he wishes as long as he's not selling it.
Amy will never buy the game herself anyway.
It's just a game; it's not anything important.
What we do in the privacy of our own homes is no one else's business.
If the company didn't want it copied, it should have protected it better.
Bill may lose his friendship with Amy if he doesn't copy the program.

Arguments against making the copy:
It's illegal to do it.
Once Bill gives it away, he has no control over it. Amy may sell or give it to a dozen others.
The author of the program has devoted long hours to producing it; she or he deserves to be paid for the work.
Why should Bill give Amy something free that he has paid for?

Following this discussion, the group should try to reach a consensus. A statement of the group's opinion should be written on the board in the form of a "We believe" statement.

Guided Practice:
Working in groups, the students will be given other scenarios of situations involving computer ethics. They will record the pros and cons, and then try to reach a consensus and write a statement expressing the group's opinion on each question.
When the groups have completed their work, a reporter from

each group will be asked to share the problem, pros and cons, and consensus with the class.

Independent Practice:
Each student will be asked to write an essay explaining his or her beliefs on computer ethics issues.

REFERENCES

Alessi, Stephen M. and Stanley R. Trollip. *Computer Based Instruction Methods and Development.* Englewood Cliffs, NJ: Prentice-Hall, 1985.

Bragaw, Donald H. and H. Michael Hartoonian. "Social Studies: The Study of People in Society." In *Content of the Curriculum,* ed. Ronald S. Brandt. Alexandria, VA: Association for Supervision and Curriculum Development, 1988.

Johnson, David W. and Roger T. Johnson. "Cooperative Learning: One Key to Computer Assisted Learning," *The Computing Teacher* 1 (October 1985): 11–12.

Myers, Lynn. "Lesson Design: Where in the U.S.A. Is Carmen Sandiego?" Unpublished paper. Iowa City, IA, January 1988.

Naisbitt, John. *Megatrends.* New York: Warner Communications, 1982.

Toffler, Alvin. *Future Shock.* New York: Random, 1970.

SOFTWARE REFERENCES

Annam. Educational Activities, Inc., Freeport, NY.

Appleworks. Apple Computer, Inc., Cupertino, CA.

Archeology Search. McGraw-Hill, New York, NY.

Demo-graphics. CONDUIT, Iowa City, IA.

Immigrant, The Irish Experience. Educational Technology Center, Harvard Graduate School, Cambridge, MA.

MECC: Graph. Minnesota Educational Computing Consortium, St. Paul, MN.

The Newsroom. Springboard Software, Inc., Minneapolis, MN.

Oregon Trail. Minnesota Educational Computing Consortium, St. Paul, MN.

The Other Side. Tom Snyder Productions, Cambridge, MA.

PFS: File. Scholastic, Inc., Jefferson City, MO.

Polls and Politics. Minnesota Educational Computing Consortium, St. Paul, MN.

The Print Shop. Broderbund Software, Inc., San Rafael, CA.

Where in Europe Is Carmen Sandiego? Broderbund Software, Inc., San Rafael, CA.

Where in the U.S.A. Is Carmen Sandiego? Broderbund Software, Inc., San Rafael, CA.

Where in the World Is Carmen Sandiego? Broderbund Software, Inc., San Rafael, CA.

Chapter 13
Using Computers in Science

For a number of years the science curriculum has placed as much emphasis on the process of science as on the facts of science. Science educators have recognized and valued the thinking processes that scientific inquiry demands, and have consequently been devising activities which encourage skills such as classification and categorization, analysis, hypothesis, synthesis, deduction, drawing of inferences, and evaluation. Whereas focusing on these "higher-order thinking skills" may be a recent development for educators in some disciplines, science teachers have long been incorporating the teaching of these skills into their presentations and activities.

Computer technology with its information processing capabilities integrates well into the scientific process model. The computer has numerous and diverse uses in the science classroom: (1) as an interactive teaching tool performing and directing simulations and addressing problem-solving strategies, (2) as a laboratory tool for collecting data, and (3) as an information manager with databases.

SIMULATIONS

The purpose of a simulation is to recreate various events, devices, or phenomena via computer. A computer simulation can provide to students a scientific experience that might otherwise be considered too expensive, too dangerous, or too time-consuming to undertake. A well-designed computer simulation can allow the science teacher to conserve expensive equipment and materials while still teaching the concept or procedure. Another advantage in simulations is that student mistakes or errors are more easily rectified: if a mistake is made, the simulation is generally salvageable, unlike in real experiments where one error can ruin the entire project. Also, it is usually somewhat easier to control variables in a computer simulation than in an actual laboratory experiment, where the risk of contamination from outside factors constantly looms. Finally, a computer simulation can provide a sound basis for further experiments (Weaver 1986). There are limitations in science simulations, however. First, unless students have been carefully primed on the particular features of the simulation, they could develop some misconceptions about the real-world situation—a false sense of reality. An animated astronomy simulation which leads elementary-age students to believe that the sun, planets, and stars revolve around the earth is reinforcing a false concept. Some simulations are simply limited by the hardware and/or software features which cannot accurately replicate the natural-world event. Frog dissection, a core laboratory procedure in most high school and some junior high biology courses, just doesn't have the same effect when carried out on a microcomputer that the real dissection offers. It may be preferable, though, to no frog dissection at all, if the actual specimens, or necessary tools and facilities, are not otherwise available. Finally, some science educators criticize simulations because "real science" is very often messy and tedious, while computer simulations gloss over that fact. They claim that simulations are misleadingly easy.

Science educators must weigh the advantages of using a particular simulation against its limitations when deciding whether to simulate or undertake the real lab. An example of a simulation which is frequently presented in biology classes is that of CATLAB, a genetic simulation which allows students to breed cats, producing genetically viable offspring, thereby demonstrating the principles of inheritance. A similar program, Heredity Dog, is slightly less complex and is appropriate for use with junior high-age students. In both simulations, students are given the opportunity to make choices, input variables, and collect, analyze, and interpret genetic data in a very short period of time. They can make predictions and test their hypotheses about inheritance factors. Without the computer simulation, this type of genetic experiment would not be feasible in secondary school science laboratories (Krajcik 1987). Even fruit flies take a relatively long time to reproduce and do not offer the variety of genetic variables that CATLAB and Heredity Dog offer.

PROBLEM-SOLVING PROGRAMS

Earlier chapters have discussed the purpose of problem solving software: to introduce and develop various thinking skills and strategies in students. Much of the software designed to promote thinking processes is lacking a relevant content; but without a heavy dose of facts, concepts, or principles to weigh down the lesson, this software frees the students to focus on a process or strategy which can then later be used with an appropriate content. Many of the thinking skills focused on in this problem-solving software can be translated to scientific practice and procedures.

An upper elementary teacher uses a problem-solving software program to extend the thinking skills introduced in a simple science experiment. The unit begins with the use of Mystery Powders (McGraw-Hill), a hands-on science activity in which students first try to determine the properties of five unlabeled white substances (sugar, salt, baking soda, starch, and plaster of Paris), eventually determining the identities of those substances given data about their reactions with water, heat, iodine, and vinegar. In the course of the activity the students learn some facts and principles about the powders, but more importantly, they learn and practice the scientific skills of observing (comparing and contrasting), drawing inferences or predicting, making a hypothesis, isolating and testing a variable (trial and error), and using data to reach a conclusion (cause and effect). They also learn and experience the importance of accurate, consistent record keeping in scientific experiments.

After the Mystery Powders activity, the teacher introduces the students to a software program, The Incredible Laboratory (Sunburst). The teacher controls the program, with the computer connected to a large-screen monitor allowing the entire class to observe and compare the creatures created by various combinations of "chemicals." As in the Mystery Powders experiment, the students must try to isolate variables and determine the cause-and-effect relationship each chemical or combination of chemicals has on the makeup of the creature. The teacher encourages the students to develop some system for recording which chemicals have been tested and the effect each seems to produce. Students discover the importance of using consistent terminology in their record keeping. After enough group experience is conducted for students to have determined how to test variables and record the results, the students go to the computer lab where they work in pairs at computers with The Incredible Laboratory (lab pack of software). Many of the students advance to higher levels of the program where the variables are combined. The teacher's role in the lab is to guide the students by asking such questions as: "What do you see?" "What did trial 1 and trial 2 have in common?" "How did you figure that out?" "What are you going to write down?"

Using the problem-solving software in this fashion extends the thinking skills used in the experiment with the powders, giving the students further practice in observing, hypothesizing, testing, and determining cause-and-effect relationships beyond the limited variable experience the simple hands-on experiment could offer. The Incredible Laboratory can deal with much more complex combinations of variables that any actual elementary-age appropriate experiment can offer.

LABORATORY TOOL

The idea behind the microcomputer-based laboratory is that by using a computer to streamline the mundane, tedious tasks of data collection, the students are released to concentrate on designing the experiment, predicting, and analyzing the results. The computer becomes a piece of laboratory equipment; sensitive devices or instruments which collect the various data are interfaced to the computer which records the data for use by the student. This type of scientific experimentation allows the student to use the same kinds of inquiry and problem-solving strategies that practicing scientists use, but which were never before possible because of the cost of the highly specialized instrumentation. Another benefit of the microcomputer-based laboratory is the ability of the computer to continue to gather data over time, something not feasible for students typically limited to science lab one period of the day. Using the computer as a laboratory tool has an advantage over on-screen computer simulations in that it is using real data from the natural world.

The microcomputer-based lab gathers data through transducers—devices which measure physical properties, and then translate the measurements into electrical currents which are computer-readable. The transducers are interfaced to the computer, often into the game port (Walton 1985). Some science teachers have made their own measuring and interfacing devices, writing their own software programs to handle the display of the data in readable terms. Other teachers use commercially produced packages which contain not only the necessary measurement devices and interfacing equipment, but also software written to display and help analyze the collected data.

An increasing amount of commercial science tool software is being marketed. One program focuses on motion: students learn basic physics concepts of velocity and acceleration by using a motion probe which allows them to graph and interpret results of movements of various objects and/or themselves. Another program uses sensitive temperature probes to investigate such scientific phenomena as heat loss and change of state. Biological programs allows students to collect data relating to brain waves and electrical activities in the heart and muscles. Few schools could afford expensive EEG and EKG equipment, but a microcomputer-based lab package affords the biology students some of the capabilities of this instrumentation.

Experiments in Human Physiology (HRM) contains temperature probes and heart rate and light sensors. The program allows students to measure and analyze data relating to their own and others' heart rate, respiration rate, skin temperature, and response time. Also included are experiments with biofeedback (skin temperature and heart rate), the effect of exercise, and psychological stress (a simplistic lie detector). High school biology students are guided to make predictions and draw conclusions based on the data collected.

Science Toolkit (Broderbund) consists of a basic Master Module and several add-on module packages. The Master Module contains standard instrumentation: a temperature probe and a light probe. The software displays the data collected by the probes using graphics; the menu-driven program has the look of a notebook. Students can conduct a number of experiments, testing various physics principles and laws using the probes and the computer's internal clock as a timer. The first Toolkit add-on module, Speed and Motion, requires the use of the Master Module devices plus additional instrumentation: a speedometer and a tachometer. Concepts such as acceleration, deceleration, and thrust can be investigated using the speedometer, while cyclical motion and momentum experiments make use of the tachometer. The module package includes photocells for triggering the internal timer, and a miniature, balloon-powered car to function as the subject in some of the experiments (Markowitz 1987).

The Voyage of the Mimi (Bank Street College) is a cross-disciplinary unit for upper elementary- and junior high-age students which uses a variety of materials including videotapes and computer programs. The video programs present the story of a group of people on a research voyage who are studying humpback whales. The computer modules involve a variety of computer applications: estimating distances using LOGO, calculating metric conversions; using interfaced devices, "sensors," to collect data about temperature, light, and sound. By using the computer modules, the students are able to replicate some of the real-life experiments they see the researchers conduct in the Mimi video program.

DATABASES

Previous chapters have discussed the use of the database as a vehicle for organizing and presenting information. Science content, perhaps more than any other in the curriculum, lends itself to database structuring and analysis.

A number of data files are being produced for use in science curricula. Scholastic has developed a series of data file programs which operate with PFS: File and deal with such areas as life science and physical science. The life science program contains an animal database which was used in a junior high life science course as the basis of an inquiry-based activity. Students working in pairs were first allowed to explore the database to discover the type and range of information it contained. They then performed guided searches of the database designed to help them practice identifying the problem, defining a search strategy, and analyzing the results. Finally, each pair devised an animal inquiry and performed the necessary search or searches to discover and confirm the results. For example, some students investigated the relationship of weight to heart rate. Others looked at fertilization method compared with litter size. The students had to report or "communicate" the results of their inquiry in one of several ways. Some students wrote the results; others presented the results orally; still others produced graphs which summarized visually what their investigations had found.

A different type of database package is GeoWorld, a Tom Snyder program which actually combines a database file of natural resources with a geological simulation. The objective of the simulation is to learn about the earth's crust and geological features and to discover the worldwide distribution patterns of the various resources. This is accomplished by performing a number of geological tests and by keeping accurate records of the evidence learned from the tests.

A special advantage of GeoWorld is that after completing a simulation, the student may save the results, the raw data from that simulation, to an Appleworks database file or word processor file. If the student creates a database file of the information gathered from the simulation, he or she has increased opportunities to study those data, manipulating them to see patterns, test hypotheses, and draw conclusions.

SUMMARY

The use of computers in the science classroom has numerous, varied applications, adding a new dimension to the scientific investigations students can conduct. The computer functions as an interactive teaching tool performing simulations and problem-solving activities; as a laboratory tool or instrument for measuring, monitoring, and analyzing data; and as an information manager through the use of databases. Because science educators place as much emphasis on the process of science as on facts, the computer as a processing tool can be integrated into many activities. The goal, then, of the science teacher is to select computer activities that truly serve to complement and enhance the science objectives, whether content or process related.

A DATABASE LESSON IN LIFE SCIENCE

What follows is a lesson that incorporates a computer activity involving a locally created database into an existing science research project. This database activity, designed for a junior high life science class, is one component of a comprehensive research project. The life science teacher and the library media specialist had previously developed and conducted a research unit to replace the usual textbook approach to the study of human diseases. The objectives of the unit included (1) introducing students to the critical facts about various human diseases and conditions, (2) reinforcing library research skills, and (3) giving students practice in formal writing techniques. Each student selected one disease, conducted library research to learn about the disease, and wrote a formal report which was first submitted in draft form, and then edited and resubmitted for evaluation.

The science teacher, recognizing the value of database skills to his students, was searching for appropriate, relevant ways to incorporate database skills into his units, so a database component was devised and integrated into the disease research unit. This database activity serves to introduce students to the various diseases and gives students relevant practice in searching a database.

The teacher created a small disease database on Appleworks that contained basic information on 25 diseases: the disease name, a definition, symptoms, and treatments. The disease database activity, "The Doctor Game," was conducted in the computer lab during the first days of the research unit. In fact, because the activity was held before students had even selected their research topics, the database activity allowed them to learn something about many of the topics before having to choose one to research in depth (Bannow and Rehmke 1988).

Lesson Plan: The Doctor Game

Materials Needed:
- Computer lab with two students per station
- Appleworks software for each station
- Disease Data File for each station
- Folders with printouts from Disease Data File

Objectives:
1. The learner will be introduced to basic facts about some human diseases.
2. The learner will practice database searching skills.
3. The learner will experience a real-world application of databases in medical diagnosis.

Lesson Input:
Discuss how a doctor goes about diagnosing a disease or condition on the basis of the symptoms a patient describes. The doctor has a "database" of diseases in his or her memory, the information "entered" into this memory database from medical school coursework, observation, and practical experience. This memory database is continually updated with new information. Sometimes, though, a doctor has difficulty in diagnosing, because the necessary data aren't in the memory

database, or because the facts just don't fit the standard pattern. Other sources of information must then be consulted—another doctor, texts, perhaps a computer database.

Guided Practice:

The students work in pairs, one assigned the role of the patient, the other the doctor. The patient has a folder that contains disease cards—printouts from the database listing the vital information about each of the diseases. The doctor has access to the disease information on the database file disk.

Round One of the game begins with the patient informing the doctor partner of a symptom the patient is experiencing, based on the information on the disease card. "Doctor, I have a headache!" The doctor then searches the database to determine which or how many diseases include "headache" as a symptom. The doctor notes other symptoms for those diseases which involve "headache," asking the patient if, for example, a fever is also present. The patient responds according to the information on the particular disease card. The doctor performs another database search, attempting to narrow down the possibilities with the addition of another symptom (headache AND fever). The doctor is awarded points for efficiency in diagnosing the disease: the fewer questions asked and searches performed, the greater number of points awarded. The students trade roles, so each partner experiences "computer diagnosis."

Succeeding rounds of "The Doctor Game" involve treatment as well as diagnosis, requiring the students to begin to remember and assimilate the information in the database.

Summary:

The outcome of this database activity is that students learn some basic facts about diseases, their symptoms, and treatment. They gain practice in manipulating a database and formulating a search strategy. Finally, the students see how the computer can function as a tool in medical diagnosis. The activity is quite simplistic, but most students are able to visualize how this type of information management procedure works in the real world.

The research unit included another database application in that students were given the opportunity to perform online database searches to locate appropriate sources of information for their reports.

REFERENCES

Bannow, Rollin and Denise Rehmke. "The Doctor Game: Data Bases in Science." Iowa Educational Media Association Spring Conference, Cedar Rapids, IA, April 1988.

Krajcik, Joseph S. and Craig Berg. "Exemplary Software for the Science Classroom." *School Science and Mathematics* 87 (October 1987): 494–500.

Manzelli, Jane A. "New Curriculum Soundings on a Voyage of the Mimi." *Computers in the Schools* 3 (1986): 55–61.

Markowitz, Mike. "Discovering Science." *A+ Magazine* 5 (July 1987): 26–39.

Walton, Karen Doyle. "Computers in the Curriculum: Science." *Electronic Learning* 4 (February 1985): 44–47.

Weaver, David and Donald Holznagel. "Integrating the Computer with Middle School/Junior High Science Instruction: The Issues." In *Computers in the Classroom,* ed. Henry S. Kepner, Jr. Washington, DC: NEA, 1986.

SOFTWARE REFERENCES

Appleworks. Apple Computer, Inc., Cupertino, CA.

CATLAB. CONDUIT, Iowa City, IA.

Experiments in Human Physiology. HRM Software, Pleasantville, NY.

GeoWorld. Tom Snyder Productions, Cambridge, MA.

Heredity Dog. HRM Software, Pleasantville, NY.

The Incredible Laboratory. Sunburst Communications, Pleasantville, NY.

Mystery Powders. McGraw-Hill, New York, NY.

PFS:File. Scholastic, Inc., Jefferson City, MO.

Science Toolkit Master Module. Broderbund, San Rafael, CA.

Science Toolkit Module 1: Speed and Motion. Broderbund, San Rafael, CA.

Voyage of the Mimi. Holt, New York, NY.

Chapter 14
Real-World Computer Applications in Elective Areas

We have stressed the importance of using computers to teach in ways that were not possible before or to teach some content better than was possible before. This concept is especially relevant in those elective and exploratory areas of the curriculum where students may now experience sophisticated applications of computer technology within the school setting. Computer-aided design and manufacturing, the use of computerized databases and spreadsheets, robotics, desktop publishing, and computer-generated music are all examples of "real-world" uses of computers which few schools would have dreamed of offering a few years ago. Yet all of these applications are now within the reach of most schools.

The intent of this chapter is to paint a broad picture of how computer technology can enhance the curriculum in elective areas common to secondary schools. Several principles are common to each of these areas:

1. The computer is in no way replacing the existing program. Instead, the integration of computer applications serves to expand and enhance the subject area.
2. Because these are specialized areas, the computer equipment used must be chosen with careful attention to the needs of the area. The specific applications to be used should be decided upon, and then the hardware which best meets the requirements of the application should be purchased.
3. Technology is affecting jobs in each of these areas. One of the goals of each of the areas should be to familiarize students with careers in the discipline and the impact of technology on those careers.

ART

A basic goal of school art programs might be stated as stimulating students "to perceive, comprehend and respond to the visual world and the visual arts" (Iowa Department of Public Instruction n.d., 17). The visual world is changing. Moviegoers are regularly amazed by new visual effects created by George Lucas and his Industrial Light and Magic Company. A local shopping mall attraction is a booth where one can purchase a digitized "photo" of one's self, created by a video camera/computer interface. Even the monthly newsletter from your local service club has recently taken on a much more "artistic" appearance. Technology is changing art and is both providing new avenues for creating art and new careers in art.

There are three major reasons for art students to be exposed to the role of the computer in the visual world:

1. The computer is a new medium for artistic expression. Television and magazines abound with examples of computer-created art. Computer art shows are commonplace. Just as photography provided a new means of creating art in the early 1900s, the computer provides a new avenue today.
2. The computer is a powerful tool for designing art which will be produced in other media. For example, a weaver might plan a piece of work first on the computer screen, where it is easy to adjust the size, change the colors or shape, and alter the pattern. Once satisfied with the plan designed and "edited" on screen, the artist can proceed to creating the actual weaving without risk of wasting precious time or expensive materials because the actual work does not live up to the artist's expectations. Using the computer in this way is analogous to writing with a word processor, since the artist can get his or her ideas down quickly on the screen, play with the image, rearrange things, and add and subtract, without the tedium of having to start from scratch each time that changes are desired. Many kinds of artists are using computers in this way to design drawings, weavings, sculpture, or other work before putting it into its final form.
3. Students need to be aware of the multitude of careers becoming available by combining art with technology. Architecture, commercial art, cinematography, advertising, and publishing are but a few areas where visual literacy and computer literacy are soundly intertwined (Mercier 1987).

Students may produce art with computers in two ways—by programming graphics in such computer languages as BASIC and by using an external input device such as a graphics tablet (see Figure

14.1). Within the art class, programming may not prove to be the most desirable alternative since it places another step between the "artist" and the creation of a piece of work. Students must first design a graphic on paper, then write the program—really a series of commands placing dots or colored blocks in various locations on the computer screen—and then "run" the program for the graphic to be created. While many beautiful and complex graphics have been created using this method, art teachers may find that students who have the skills required to do programming may not possess the aesthetic sense required to create art and vice versa.

FIGURE 14.1. Using a Graphics Tablet as an Input Device to Create a Drawing

The second method of producing computer-generated art will feel more familiar to art instructors as students simply use an input device to draw an image which then appears on the computer screen. Examples of such devices would be the Apple Graphics Tablet or the simpler and less expensive Koala Pad, where the student uses a stylus to "draw" an image on a board which is wired with tiny electronic sensors. The image being drawn appears simultaneously on the computer screen. Such drawing requires students to practice a different type of eye-hand coordination than that normally used in drawing; rather than watching one's hand as it actually does the drawing, the student must watch the computer screen while his or her hand operates in a different area usually to one side of the computer. A great advantage of drawing in this medium, especially for young artists, is that mistakes can be quickly and easily corrected, thus encouraging more experimentation than might take place if students are working with paints or ink. Students can also print out their designs, even if only in black and white, and either add color to the printout or use the printout as a basis for making revisions. Disadvantages include the fact that detail cannot always be done as finely on a graphics input device, and the sensitive electronics involved may prove difficult to keep in good repair when usage is heavy.

Computers such as the Apple IIGS with its excellent color resolution will prove to be a boon to computerized art in the public schools. Using the Apple's "mouse" as an input device, and graphics software such as Deluxe Paint II from Electronic Arts, students can create pictures in an almost infinite range of colors. Other features of the software include the ability to isolate, enlarge, and work on a small section of a picture, then put it back into the whole. A series of pictures created in this way may be saved to disk and presented as a "slide show" of computer generated art. Such a slide show might be considered to be the final product of a student's efforts with the computer. It is also possible to print out the pictures in color, using either a colored ribbon or more sophisticated ink jet printers or plotting devices. Art teachers are also experimenting with animation software and with digitizers, devices which use a video camera to take a picture which then appears as a digitized image on the computer screen. Students can take this digitized image and modify it to create a new picture.

MUSIC

The possible uses of computers in music closely parallel those in art. The computer is being used as a new tool for creating music and it is dramatically changing the way music is produced professionally. One or two musicians can now produce the sounds of an entire orchestra using a series of computer-controlled instruments including synthesizers, drum machines and digital pianos. Compact disks and digital audio tapes are produced using computerized processes (Bateman 1987).

In schools, the computer can be used to create music either by itself using one of the many software packages available for this purpose or in conjunction with another musical device, usually an electronic keyboard. We have compared creating art with a computer to writing with a word processor. This same analogy applies to music as the student goes through the process of getting ideas, putting them down on paper in the form of musical notation, revising and refining the composition and, finally, performing the work for an audience. Once again, using the computer to complete this process makes it less tedious than composing in the traditional way, and thus makes the student feel freer to experiment and be creative.

There are many software packages available which allow students to compose music. The best of them are designed to operate on the Commodore Amiga which is capable of 4-voice stereo output, and on the Apple IIGS, which has a 15-voice capacity and a built-in analog-to-digital converter (Bateman 1987). One such example is Activision's Music Studio which has comprehensive composing capabilities that let the student use a mouse to drag color-coded notes into the desired position on a staff (see Figure 14.2). Compositions can be done in classical, rock, or jazz modes, and simulated vocals can be added (McClain 1987).

A second way of creating music with a computer is to connect a microcomputer to an electronic keyboard. This is made possible by a system known as MIDI, or musical instrument digital interface, which is a set of standardized specifications for connecting electronic music devices to each other and to computers. By connecting a keyboard to a computer, students can learn to play and to compose on the keyboard while the computer monitors their progress, provides needed prompts, and serves as a recording device to save the student's work.

STUDENT PUBLICATIONS

The microcomputer is affecting nearly every aspect of the production of student publications. The typing, revising, and editing of student writing has been done with word processors for a number of years. High school journalism departments have kept mailing lists and printed mailing labels with database software. Spreadsheet programs are used to keep track of accounts and billing for advertising.

The authors of this book have been careful not to make extravagant claims for the potential of computers to drastically alter education. However, the advent of desktop publishing to the school journalism program does constitute a revolutionary change. Those of us with experience on high school newspapers will remember the laborious process of typing stories, editing and often retyping, counting headlines, taking or sending copy to a distant typesetting location, and pasting up copy and headlines when they returned from the

FIGURE 14.2. Using The Music Studio to Compose Music with a Computer

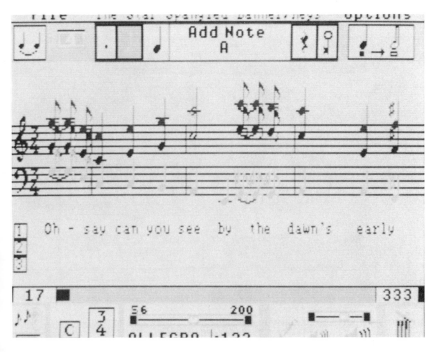

Reprinted by permission of Activision, Inc., Mountain View, CA.

typesetter. This process has continued with relatively little change for nearly 50 years. The newspaper produced in this way often contained news that was out-of-date before it was printed.

Desktop publishing effectively eliminates the middle step—that of typesetting—in the production process. Using a computer, special software, and a laser printer, student journalists can create on-screen, sophisticated layouts, including headlines and graphics. They can then incorporate text into these layouts and print camera-ready copy in regular or tabloid size (see Figure 14.3). This copy can then be taken, or sent via modem, to the offset printing press.

Desktop publishing offers several advantages over conventional methods of preparing student publications:

1. Design capabilities. As with programs used to create art, desktop publishing offers greater flexibility to students in designing graphics and lettering or headlines. Images designed using graphics software can be easily altered, enlarged or reduced, and stored for later use (Jordan 1987). Desktop publishing allows the student to work on a "what

FIGURE 14.3. A Desktop Publishing System Sample Layout, Using PageMaker

Used by permission of the software developer, Aldus Corporation, Seattle, WA.

you see is what you get" (WYSIWYG) basis, where before the student could only imagine what the final product would look like once all the pieces—art, text, and headlines—came together.

2. Control. Desktop publishing puts control and ownership of the publication in the hands of the students. They are responsible for the design of the finished product rather than someone at a distant printing shop. Student creativity need not be limited by the column width and type sizes dictated by the typesetting equipment used by the print shop. Such control also enables students to catch errors in the production stage that might not have been noticed until page proofs or final copy was received. Such errors can then be corrected without added expense.

3. Cost. While the start-up costs associated with desktop publishing are high, schools will save money on typesetting and graphics. One medium-sized high school estimated savings of about $2,000 per year on the publication costs of its yearbook alone (Jordan 1987).

4. Real-world methodologies. Graphic artists in all areas are using desktop publishing as an everyday tool. Journalists have used computerized equipment for many years. At rela-

tively low cost, students can learn skills on equipment that closely approximates that used in business.

Publications advisers have identified some limitations of desktop publishing equipment. Considerable concern has been expressed over the quality of print available with a laser printer which outputs 300 dots per inch as opposed to the 1,200-plus dots per inch of traditional typesetting equipment. Those of us accustomed to the 70 to 80 dots per inch of the standard dot matrix printer will probably be well-satisfied with laser printer quality! Publications advisers also caution that desktop publishing is not a time-saver; consideration must be given to the fact that learning to use the system and software will take time, and each new group of student journalists will need to be trained.

The Apple Macintosh computer is the current standard in desktop publishing, although IBM has recently begun to gain ground. The minimum equipment needed to set up a desktop publishing operation would be two Macintosh computers with a hard disk drive (the hard disk speeds up the complicated operations of the software and helps avoid constant disk swapping) and a laser printer. Required software includes a quality word processing program such as Microsoft Word, a page layout program such as Aldus's PageMaker (also available for the IBM System 2) or Letraset's Ready, Set, Go! and a graphics program such as MacDraw or SuperPaint. Such a system would cost in the neighborhood of $9,000 but could be expected to pay for itself in about three years with savings in newspaper and yearbook publications costs. It is likely that most high school publications departments would need to add additional Macintosh stations depending upon the number of students involved in publications (Jordan 1987).

INDUSTRIAL ARTS/INDUSTRIAL TECHNOLOGY

Some of the most dramatic examples of "real-world" computer applications made possible by the microcomputer occur in the area of industrial arts, now being renamed Industrial Technology in many school districts. Students can design products using sophisticated computerized drafting programs, program robots to perform work, and produce products on computer-controlled machine tools. Traditionally, the industrial arts curriculum has offered a variety of classes designed to help students understand industrial processes including design, mass production, power and energy, and research and development. Several areas of this traditional curriculum lend themselves to the use of microcomputers (Figure 14.4):

1. Planning and designing products. Computer-aided design (CAD) and computer-aided design and drafting (CADD) have become buzzwords in industry and in industrial technology. Using a microcomputer program, drafting students can draw on screen, using a mouse or other input device, sophisticated plans for buildings or products. Use of CADD in designing products has the same advantages described earlier when using computers to aid in artistic design was discussed: more experimentation, and hence, greater creativity, is likely to result when the student can easily make changes in on-screen designs without the pain of having to start over from scratch. A CAD-equipped microcomputer can also be connected to a machine which utilizes "computer numerical control" or CNC to produce the product the student has designed on screen, allowing the student to simulate computer-aided manufacture (CAM) as well. Both of these processes are commonly used in business.

2. Robotics. A robot might be simply defined as a computer-controlled device that can move (Neighbors and Slaton 1987). Robots are used in manufacturing to perform many of the dull, repetitive tasks involved in mass production. In the industrial arts classroom, relatively inexpensive robots, interfaced with microcomputers, can be programmed to perform different demonstrations, from having a robot "arm" move an object from one place to another to having robots equipped with sensing devices change direction or operations as a result of some input received via voice or through contact with an external object. One goal of using robots is to create an awareness in students of the principles involved in using robots and of the basic issues involving automation in industry; the use of a robot in the classroom can make these abstract issues more concrete for students.

3. Graphic arts. Design, drawing and lettering, and the printing process are included in many high school industrial arts programs. Many such programs produce posters, pamphlets, and newsletters for school activities and sometimes for the school district. Desktop publishing, as described above in the section on student publications, is of obvious importance here. Just as they do in the journalism classes described above, students can use a microcomputer, equipped with such software as PageMaker, and a laser printer to take the production of graphic arts projects such as pamphlets and posters to the point of final printing.

4. "Principles of Technology" classes. Many schools are offering an introductory class, often titled "Principles of Technology" or "Introduction to Technology," to familiarize stu-

dents with the role of technology in industry. Such a class, sometimes referred to as an applied physics course, is designed to give students an understanding of how technology, including computers, affects traditional industrial arts areas such as energy and power, production and construction, research and development, and construction and transportation.

FIGURE 14.4. Computers in the Industrial Technology Classroom

A wealth of microcomputer-driven equipment is available to schools for use in industrial technology programs. IBM- and Macintosh-based CAD capabilities more closely approximate those used in industry, but schools which possess Apple II equipment can utilize relatively inexpensive software such as Versacad's Entry-Level CADApple or CADdraw from Kitchen Sink Software. CADApple and other software becoming available for the Apple IIGS will take advantage of the excellent graphics capabilities of that machine. Other equipment required for computer-aided drafting includes an input device such as a mouse or graphics tablet and a pen plotter, since technical drawings require much finer, sharper lines than can be provided by either dot matrix or laser printers. In an article in the January 1988, *A+ Magazine,* it was estimated that a school should be able to establish a CAD lab for about $1,000 per station, using Apple II equipment and having several stations share a plotter (Markowitz 1988).

Of course, much more sophisticated systems are available, including some which integrate CAD with CNC milling or drilling machines and/or lathes. Such systems may also utilize robots to load a product from one machine to another. While such systems are costly, they enable the student to experience the computer-aided manufacturing process from beginning to end.

BUSINESS EDUCATION

One traditional goal of business education has been to prepare students to assume clerical and secretarial positions in the work force. Students were trained to be fast and accurate typists and took courses in document preparation, office practice, consumer economics, and sometimes bookkeeping and accounting. Many of these classes placed strong emphasis on good basic skills in reading, writing, listening, speaking, and interpersonal communications; these are all qualities still considered highly desirable by employers.

Since most offices now utilize automation in some form, business education programs are changing to incorporate concepts necessary for workers to function in a high-tech environment. The "big three" applications of computer technology—word processing, databases, and spreadsheets—are all appropriate for inclusion in the high school business education curriculum.

Word processing is the basic method of document production in offices. Instruction in word processing in business education classes goes far beyond what students may encounter in earlier keyboarding/ word processing instruction. Students will learn sophisticated assembly and editing functions, methods for building tables and indexes, file and disk management, and the use of a spelling checker program. Another valuable skill, seldom taught in other areas, is the use of the documentation that accompanies a software package (Nardone 1987).

Database management programs are essential tools for organizing and retrieving information in an office setting. Databases may contain student records, sales information on each of a firm's customers, medical records, inventories, or any information that must be recorded in an organized fashion. Database programs can also be merged with word processing programs to produce the sort of personalized form letters that we all frequently receive in the mail, and to produce mailing lists and labels.

The basic purpose of a spreadsheet is to organize numerical information in useful ways. Spreadsheets can be used to keep budgets and accounts and are most useful in making projections since various elements can be electronically manipulated. For example, in predicting profits on a new product, the unit price and quantity produced might be manipulated to find the most advantageous combination. Spreadsheets can also be used to generate useful tables and graphs for demonstration purposes. Businesses commonly use a software which combines all three of these applications; examples of such integrated packages are Appleworks, Lotus 1,2,3 and Microsoft Works.

Other areas of concern to those training students for office work include electronic mail, telecommunications, and desktop publishing. Office workers are now sending both interoffice and long-distance memos via the computer, thus eliminating the need for paper copies unless someone wishes to have one. In that case, he or she can simply activate the printer attached to the computer. Telecommunications applications such as accessing stock prices and other information sources via telephone modem are discussed in Chapter 10. Desktop publishing, described elsewhere in this chapter, will be used to produce a variety of office projects including the company newsletter and the various brochures and pamphlets produced in any office.

Business educators are training workers for jobs that will change several times during their working years (Cetron 1985). For this reason, it is essential that students have a thorough understanding of the concepts involved in using the various types of equipment and applications software they will encounter. They must have an understanding of how information is managed by computers, as well as the ability to troubleshoot or analyze problems they may encounter in using equipment and software. While much training will necessarily take place after a student is hired for a particular position, those who have a basic understanding of how computers and software work will assimilate such training much more readily.

Business educators need to develop a dialog with local business to determine specific training needs. Business education classrooms should be equipped with machines that most closely approximate those used in business; at the present time, that would mean IBM or IBM-compatible equipment. Consideration should also be given to networking the equipment in the lab and to allowing the network to access a laser printer; this is a common configuration in offices.

SUMMARY

Special needs in elective areas of the curriculum, particularly in high schools, will necessitate the purchase of special-purpose computer equipment. Students enrolling in these areas will have the opportunity to use real-world design and production methods which were not available to the school curriculum before microcomputers. Providing students with experience using the new tools of technology is an important component of both computer literacy and career awareness.

REFERENCES

Bateman, Selby. "The New Music." *Compute!* 9 (May 1987): 18–20.

Cetron, Marvin. *Schools of the Future: How American Business and Education Can Cooperate to Save Our Schools.* New York: McGraw-Hill, 1985.

Iowa Department of Public Instruction. *The Visual Arts in Iowa Schools.* Des Moines: Department of Public Instruction, n.d.

Jordan, Jim. "FROM THE DESKTOP: Why Desktop Publishing?" *Scholastic Editor's Trends in Publications* 67:1 (September 1987): 4–5.

Markowitz, Mike. "Entry Level CADApple." *A+ Magazine* 6 (January 1988): 73–78.

McClain, Larry. "A+ All-Stars: Music." *A+ Magazine* 5 (December 1987): 82–92.

Mercier, Nan, Iowa City School Art Coordinator. Interview, 4 December 1987, Coralville, IA.

Nardone, Virginia E. "Updating the Course in Word/Information Processing." *Business Education Forum* 41 (March 1987): 9–11.

Neighbors, David and Frank Slaton. "Robots in My Classroom?" *The Computing Teacher* 14 (March 1987): 24–28.

SOFTWARE REFERENCES

Appleworks. Apple Computer, Inc., Cupertino, CA.

CADApple. Versacad Corp., Huntington Beach, CA.

CADdraw. Kitchen Sink Software, Westerville, OH.

Deluxe Paint II. Electronic Arts, San Mateo, CA.

Entry Level CADApple. Versacad Corp., Huntington Beach, CA.

Lotus 1, 2, 3. Lotus Development Corp., Cambridge, MA.

MacDraw. Apple Computer, Inc., Cupertino, CA.

Microsoft Word. Microsoft Corp., Redmond, CA.

Microsoft Works. Microsoft Corp., Redmond, CA.

The Music Studio. Activision, Inc., Mountain View, CA.

PageMaker. Aldus Corp., Seattle, WA.

Ready, Set, Go! Letraset, Paramus, NJ.

SuperPaint. Silicon Beach Software, San Diego, CA.

Part III
Final
Considerations

Chapter 15
The Computer as a Tool for the School

Many of the applications described in the preceding chapters as important tools for students can also be utilized by teachers, administrators, library media specialists, and counselors to assist with the many record-keeping and paperwork responsibilities associated with operating today's school. Such applications often provide more efficient and more versatile methods of accomplishing day-to-day tasks, and can result in improved education for students.

TEACHER UTILITIES

One step toward making teachers feel comfortable with the computer as a teaching tool is to assist them in learning to use it as a personal tool. Each school should provide a place where teachers can work with computers to preview software, prepare materials, plan lessons which involve computers, and learn to use various applications.

Word processing is an essential skill for teachers, as it is for students. Teachers proficient at word processing will use the computer to write course syllabi and prepare classroom materials. Word processing provides an ideal means to prepare and store lesson plans, which can then be easily modified based upon the teacher's evaluation of the lesson. In addition, teachers can prepare novel and attractive worksheets using the graphics programs and attractive font styles now available. A teacher work area should be equipped with a machine similar to the Macintosh or Apple IIGS; teachers can take advantage of the added power of such a machine for record keeping and can generate attractive, readable overhead transparencies and handouts using its graphics capabilities. It is likely that such computers, equipped with drawing or desktop publishing software, will replace the ubiquitous primary typewriter for the preparation of overheads and the creation of worksheets.

Many teachers find it useful to keep student records on a grading program such as MECC's Grade Manager. Those comfortable with spreadsheet programs have also used them to store grades. Either type of computerized record keeping offers several advantages over computing grades from the traditional grade book. The computer is able to calculate averages, means, and standard deviations much more rapidly than can be done by hand (see Figure 15.1). It is also possible

FIGURE 15.1. Using a Computerized Grade Management Program to Compute Averages and Other Statistics

to use the computer to print out periodic "personalized" reports for students, such as at midterm time. It should be noted, however, that most teachers find it necessary to continue to record student grades in the traditional grade book, which is more portable, and often more accessible, than a computer. While this may seem like needless duplication, the use of the computer eliminates the need for the teacher to calculate each student's grades, ensures greater accuracy, and gives additional statistical information to the teacher for use in evaluating the grading system itself.

The use of test generation programs has also proved to be helpful to many teachers. The teacher develops a set of questions keyed to the objectives of each unit. The desired number of test questions can then be randomly selected by the computer, or individually selected by the teacher, and printed out in the desired order. This allows for easy revision and printing and has obvious advantages when teachers desire different versions of the test for different classes or for makeup purposes. Most test-generation programs allow for true/false, multiple choice, matching, and short answer questions (Stanton 1987). Some programs allow for the student to take the test at the computer; while the advantage here is that the test can then be automatically scored, unless computer time is plentiful, this does not seem the best instructional use of the computer. Some companies also sell data disks of test questions. It is essential that the teacher examine the questions carefully and use only those which are specifically covered in a given school's curriculum. It is probably better for teachers, perhaps working on a districtwide level, to develop their own database of test questions geared to local curricula.

Computerized test-scoring machines are also in use in many schools. These machines use an optical scanner to read students' marks on special test forms, similar to those used on most standardized tests. The machine will score the test and generate appropriate grading information such as mean and median and the most frequently missed items. While supplies can be expensive, scoring tests this way can save teacher time and provide useful information which may help the teacher in evaluating course content.

For teachers to be avid and proficient computer users, a friendly and supportive computing environment must be established. The building computer coordinator or computer aide should be available to assist teachers in learning to use applications software. Computers and software should be available for teacher checkout. Computer companies such as Apple and IBM sponsor educator plans whereby teachers can purchase computer equipment at substantial savings. Schools should promote and publicize these plans and facilitate teacher purchase of computers. Such support will pay educational dividends to the schools; computer-using teachers are daily discovering ways to accomplish classroom-related work more efficiently and to prepare materials that are more effective as well as more attractive. Such discoveries will benefit students. Computer-competent teachers possess a distinct edge over their non-computer-using colleagues.

THE COMPUTER AS AN ADMINISTRATIVE TOOL

The computer has had a profound effect on the way the administrative functions associated with running a school district are performed. In the area of financial services, a school district has the same needs as any business organization Careful budgeting records must be maintained, the ordering and receiving of materials must be recorded and accounts maintained for items purchased, inventories must be kept, and payrolls must be met. Schools also have a number of administrative responsibilities that businesses do not. These include the scheduling of students into classes, maintenance of student records, and grade reporting. For many years, these administrative functions have been computerized in most districts through the use of a time-share system on an area basis, or in some cases by individual districts maintaining their own mini- or mainframe computers.

The microcomputer can also be an important tool for the school administrator. Indeed, a 1987 survey by *Electronic Learning* showed that 71 percent of school administrators use microcomputers for some management tasks. The most common use noted in the study was for word processing, but attendance, budgeting, inventory management, and test scoring also rated highly (Barbour 1987).

The "big three" applications referred to previously—word processing, databases, and spreadsheets—can all be used profitably by the school administrator. Word processing can greatly enhance many of the typing tasks done in most offices. Form letters to parents can be customized by the addition of the individual parents' names and the inclusion of the student's name within the text. Such letters can be stored as templates and then brought up and modified as the situation demands. Many memos to staff, such as requests for budget input or year-end procedures, are used annually with only minor changes; these can be stored on disk for easy reproduction at the appropriate times. Policies and procedures manuals, and teacher and student handbooks, which undergo frequent revision, can be entered and stored on disks for easy access and changing. Correspondence maintained on disk eliminates the need for paper copies to be made and filed.

Databases provide a second powerful tool for the school office. If the information to be included in the database is planned for carefully, it can be used to fill any number of needs. For example, if health records are included, the school office can generate a list of students with hearing problems for teachers so that the students could be seated appropriately within the classroom. Mailing lists and stick-on mailing labels could be generated from the database so that only those students enrolled in foreign language or those who participate in athletics would be selected. In setting up a database for the school, a flexible system should be chosen that can be tailored to the individual building's needs. The needs of an elementary school may be different from those of the high school. Care should also be taken that data need be entered only once to serve the needs of the building; the data should be accessible by and useful to administrators, counselors, and teachers. And while making information as accessible as possible is desirable, protecting the privacy of student records must also be a priority.

Databases can also be used by administrators for other record keeping-tasks. Some schools use microcomputer-based programs to keep daily attendance records. Equipment, textbook, and supplies inventories can be maintained in a database. Records of projects for district physical plant employees might be maintained on a database; the database could be used to schedule such projects and record their completion. Over time, such record keeping would allow administrators to have a more accurate picture of the amount of time needed to perform certain projects, and hence the number of people required to maintain the district physical plant. A personnel database might be used to identify those employees who are due for physical exams or who need to take additional coursework for recertification. The district's substitute teacher list, sorted by the grade level or subject areas for which the substitutes are qualified, is a useful tool. Information in a database on professional travel, including amounts of money spent and the relationship of the travel to district goals, can improve decision making in this area.

Spreadsheets can also be used by the building or district-level administrator as a decision-making tool. Spreadsheets allow the user to manipulate numerical data to make projections based on "what if"-type questions. For example, a district administrator might predict what next year's budget would look like if teachers receive a 5 percent raise, if they receive a 6 percent raise, etc. Or the administrator might predict what next year's revenues would be if the district has 200 more students, 300 more students, or 200 fewer students. The computer can easily perform these calculations, which allow the administrator to plan more easily for any eventuality. Building administrators can also use the spreadsheet to project and maintain financial records.

Most sophisticated spreadsheets have the capability of generating charts and graphs based on the data recorded (see Figure 15.2); such visuals can greatly increase the "understandability" of large chunks of information when the administrator is required to give a presentation to the school board or district staff.

A final application becoming increasingly popular with administrators is desktop publishing, described in some detail in Chapter 14. Schools are called upon to produce a myriad of printed materials including student handbooks, programs for performances, forms, surveys, brochures, and periodic newsletters. Desktop publishing software can allow the school to create professional-looking publications within the school setting. Desktop publishing requires the use of a laser printer; while such printers are currently an expensive item, like much computer-related technology, they are declining in price. A laser printer would also enable the school office to produce near typeset-quality letters and memos.

The *Electronic Learning* (*EL*) survey cited earlier reported that IBM or IBM-compatible computers were the machine of choice for most administrative uses (Barbour 1987). Apple's Macintosh is also

FIGURE 15.2. Using Data Stored on a Spreadsheet to Generate Graphs and Charts

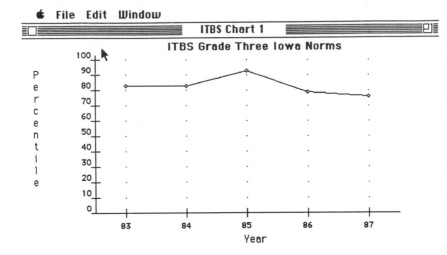

chosen frequently as an office machine due both to the power of the machine and to the ease with which administrators and staff can learn to use it. No clear software leaders emerged from the *EL* study, but integrated packages such as Lotus 1,2,3, often used in business, or Microsoft Works are frequent choices. Such packages provide word processing, database, and spreadsheet capabilities integrated into one program, making it necessary to learn one set of commands and one system of operating rather than several.

For complex routines such as payroll, scheduling, and grade reporting, which are beyond the capacity of the microcomputer, administrators will need to continue to rely on shared-time systems. However, the micro does have a place in the school office as a clerical, record-keeping, and decision-making tool. One configuration which combines the best of both worlds is to use microcomputers which can be interfaced with the larger system via modem when needed.

A TOOL FOR THE LIBRARY MEDIA CENTER

Computers are particularly good at routine, repetitive tasks and record keeping. Such tasks are essential in the school library media center and, indeed, sometimes consume a disproportionate amount of the media center staff's time. The computer has the potential to greatly reduce the time spent on routines such as filing circulation and catalog cards, typing overdue notices, and preparing statistical reports; the time saved can more profitably be spent on working with students and teachers. The speed and efficiency with which students and teachers can access the materials in the library collection can also be increased when library routines are computerized.

Circulation

The automated circulation system is the most common library management application of computer technology in schools today. Such systems use a microcomputer to check books out and in for students and teachers. Each item in the library collection is labeled with a bar code unique to that item; this system is similar to that used in grocery stores. Each library user also has his or her own bar code, usually affixed to a card and stored at the library circulation desk. Items are checked out and in by scanning the bar code with a light pen connected to the computer (see Figure 15.3).

The use of a computerized system has several advantages over manual circulation of library materials:

1. Cards for each item checked out no longer have to be filed at the end of each day, and then pulled and replaced in the book when it is returned. It has been estimated that computerizing this process saves 45 minutes for every 50 books circulated (Everhart n.d.).
2. Overdue notices are generated automatically by the computer. Students can be sent individual notices, or alphabetical lists can be generated for each homeroom. If fines are charged, they can be computed by the system and included on the overdue notice. Students with overdue materials can also be flagged by the computer to prevent them from checking out further materials until overdues are taken care of.
3. Students can stop at the circulation desk to see a list of items they have checked out. The records of students who are leaving school can easily be checked to determine if they have library materials.
4. Inventory of the library collection can be done using the light pen or portable scanning device to record each item on the shelf. The computer then generates a list of missing items. Inventory is a procedure often neglected in school libraries due to lack of staff time; computerizing this process can provide for greater accuracy in library records and greater accountability for materials.

The Card Catalog

The library card catalog is a technology that has remained virtually unchanged in the 110 years since Melvil Dewey developed his

FIGURE 15.3. A Light Pen, Used to Read Bar Codes on Library User Card, Book, and Command List

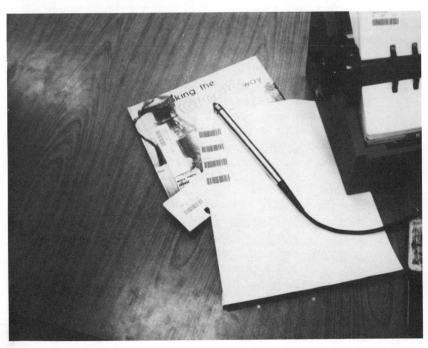

system for classifying books. Hundreds of hours are spent by library staff in preparing and filing cards in the card catalog, which most people find to be a cumbersome tool at best. Users are placed in the position of having to guess at the most appropriate subject heading to describe the topic they are researching; if accurate cross-references have not been maintained users may reach a dead end when looking under "Car" instead of "Automobile" or "Popular Music" instead of "Music, Popular." Subject headings also change from time to time; for example, titles formerly listed under "Eskimo" are now listed under the subject heading "Inuit," which is that group's preferred designation; one must look in both places to get all of the titles on this subject. Such problems may be frustrating for adults but can be incomprehensible to students. Computerizing the card catalog has many of the same time-saving advantages associated with automated circulation, but it also has the capability of greatly increasing the ease with which we can access information.

Chapter 9 discussed online searching and the use of keyword and Boolean searching strategies. Such techniques apply to the use of a computerized card catalog as well. Say, for example, that a student needs information on AIDS. Typing the word "AIDS" into a computerized catalog which allows keyword searching would result in the student finding all library materials which had "AIDS" as part of the title or as a subject heading. It would also find materials where AIDS was mentioned in any notes on the card. Other searching options allow users to expand or limit a search in a number of ways. For example, a teacher might want all of the information on AIDS and children published after 1987. A printer connected to the public access terminals would allow the teacher to print a list of such resources. This same process also allows library staff to generate quickly very specific bibliographies for users.

Once the teacher or student has located the desired material in the online card catalog, the computer will also indicate the status of that item, since the card catalog and circulation systems will operate from the same database. The student can see if the book in question has been checked out or not; if it has been checked out, the student can see when it is due to be returned.

Computerizing circulation and card catalog functions can also aid the library media specialist in making decisions about the library collection. Reports can be generated to indicate the percentage of the collection in various categories—e.g., fiction, U.S. history, sports, health. These percentages can then be compared with the circulation figures for each category, and can be analyzed in light of the curriculum of the particular school program. Most school library collections are relatively small; computerizing the catalog of library holdings will improve the ability to access all of the information in school library collections, allowing us to maximize the use of the resources we have.

Many other library routines can be enhanced through the use of the computer, even if the library does not have automated circulation and card catalog systems. The area of cataloging and preparing library materials provides one example. Most libraries buy materials preprocessed; that is, catalog cards, spine labels, and Mylar book covers are included with the book when it arrives. However, there is always a certain percentage of materials, especially nonprint items, that are not available preprocessed. These items must be cataloged and processed by the district cataloger, or if no central cataloging exists, by the school media specialist. This is a time-consuming task which can be done on the computer with the aid of a software package such as Follett's Quick Card. This program presents a template for the librarian to fill in with the assigned call number, title, author and publishing information, subject heading, and other information. The program then generates the necessary number of catalog cards with the information listed in the proper format. This can be accomplished on the standard Apple IIe or on an IBM-compatible computer linked to a printer.

Word processing and database programs have many applications in the library media center. Word processing can be used to type the many letters, memos, and lists produced in the library. Databases can be used to maintain information such as a community resource list of people and businesses willing to donate time to the schools. Databases can be used to keep track of equipment and supplies inventories, and in schools without computerized circulation, they can reduce at least somewhat the amount of time spent on overdue notices.

Many new applications of technology to libraries are on the horizon. In the future, we will see school libraries tied together via networking systems that will allow them to search each other's collections and request materials via electronic mail. Purchasing of new materials will be accomplished by typing orders on the school's computer, sending the order over the phone to the district business office, which will supply the various authorizations, and arrange for billing to the proper accounts. The Baker and Taylor Company, a well-known book jobber, already accepts orders placed electronically. Decision makers must include school library automation in their planning; it will reap a dual benefit in freeing library staff to devote more time to working with students and teachers, and in providing better access to information for everyone.

SUMMARY

Microcomputer technology enables us to perform many of the routine duties associated with operating the school in a more efficient manner. Even more importantly, it improves our ability to manage and use all of the information available to us within the school setting. Just as computer skills are essential for today's students, so are they for teachers and administrators.

REFERENCES

Barbour, Andrew. "Office Romance: Why Administrators Are Hooked on Technology." *Electronic Learning* 6 (April 1987): 18–23.
Everhart, Nancy. "Time Saved with Computerization." Crystal Lake, IL: Follett Software Company, n.d.
Stanton, David. "Testing the Test Makers." *A+ Magazine* 5 (October 1987): 57–62.

SOFTWARE REFERENCES

Grade Manager. Minnesota Educational Computing Consortium, St. Paul, MN.
Lotus 1, 2, 3. Lotus Development Corp., Cambridge, MA.
Microsoft Works. Microsoft Corp., Redmond, CA.
Quick Card. Follett Software Co., Crystal Lake, IL.

Chapter 16:
Trends and Issues in Instructional Computing

Dreams of high-tech classrooms conjure up images of students plugged into machines in a rather asocial classroom setting or a home learning environment. While those images can be exciting, what this chapter will deal with is the near and realistic future. What trends will affect education? What issues do educators need to be addressing now?

DECISION MAKING

One important construct of this book has been the idea that we must look at what tasks we need to accomplish as educators and then decide which of those is better accomplished with technological assistance. Clearly, not all content and not all objectives are best met by having students interact with technology. Decision making based on understanding of content, understanding of learning processes, and understanding of children and young adults can guide educators to use technology to its best advantage and opt for other strategies as appropriate.

Educators have an embarrassing history of adopting the latest fads, trying to make those fads meet all needs, becoming dissatisfied because the new idea did not bring success in every application, and so abandoning the innovation and moving on to the next. Examples include behavioral objectives, mastery learning, educational television, phonics, "new math," language laboratories, and criterion-referenced testing. While none of these innovations was a panacea to educational concerns, each probably had a right place in instruction and each could create better learning. The success of innovation is dependent on sound decision making, on looking at the potential applications of the innovation, studying the current status, comparing needs and capabilities, and selecting where that innovation fits best. So it is with the microcomputer. It clearly has specific capabilities.

Examples of these capabilities have been described throughout this book. On the other hand, there are teaching needs that are met more effectively and/or more efficiently without microcomputers. Some would cite teaching children to read as an example; creating a piece of instructional software to teach students how to use the Palmer method for handwriting might be cited as another example of poor utilization of this mode of instruction. Whatever the example, the point is, educators need to look at what they know about teaching and learning, about curriculum and students, and take all factors into account in deciding when to use a computer and when not. If this kind of decision making does not occur, we can look for instructional computing to never reach its potential in areas where it really can do an instructional task better than any other mode because we will have disenfranchised teachers who saw no benefit when misusing the technology. And we will be allocating limited resources to too many tasks for too many students for too little time to make a difference. Indeed, there are those who are already concerned about the waning interest in instructional computing and the decline in financial support for microcomputers. The issue of deciding what the microcomputer can do well is an important one if the equipment is not to end up in garage sales in the next decade.

SPECIALIZATION

Early in the microcomputer's school history, there was a tendency to purchase equipment of like configuration throughout a school or district. The biggest consideration was whether to buy color or monochrome monitors. Increasingly, both hardware and software are becoming more specialized. Educators have more and more options for selecting specialized equipment for specific applications. A standard machine may not travel so quickly and easily from department to department as was once the case. Obvious examples of this include such applications as computer-aided drafting, desktop publishing, scientific instrumentation, online database searching, and music synthesizing. In each curricular area, teachers will be identifying the ways a microcomputer can be adapted to meet their needs. In each instance the specifications of the equipment coupled with carefully selected software will result in department-specific equipment. To prepare for this, professional organizations in each content area need to be providing conference sessions related to this issue. Special hardware and special software for each discipline should be the topic of conference sessions. Teachers need opportunities through workshops and continuing education to learn about the application of this technology to their own domain (Spitzer 1987).

CD-ROM

CD-ROM (compact disc—read-only memory) is one technology that calls for specialization of hardware. CD-ROM is similar to the disc designed for digital audio playback. CD-ROM is a laser disc 4.72 inches in diameter; it can hold up to 250,000 pages of information and is designed for optical playback. Software written specific to CD-ROM and designed to operate with a specific computer serves as the interface between a CD-ROM player and a computer to facilitate rapid access to information stored on the disc. Although standards are emerging, not every CD-ROM disc player is compatible with every CD-ROM software package. So, districts must decide whether to wait until standards are established or must carefully scrutinize software currently available to determine whether it can improve a process and then purchase hardware to match it.

Although still images can be placed on CD-ROM, it is primarily a text medium. As such, it has its greatest potential in library media centers when students are seeking printed information. The storage capacity, searching capabilities, rapid accessibility, and durability of the compact disc are attractive features. Contents of an entire encyclopedia are contained on a single compact disc along with an extensive index that allows searchers to access each occurrence of a keyword or combination of keywords. All of this can happen within seconds. Periodical indexes, public access catalogs, indexes of books in print, and specialized databases are examples of other information available on a subscription basis with updates replacing discs (Vandergrift 1987). Because the search for information on a compact disc occurs in-house without the expense of online charges, students can search using Boolean logic without time and money concerns. The question to ask is, "Is CD-ROM a better way to meet this need for information?"

VIDEODISC

Although the videodisc has been available since the late 1970s, it is still a relatively new technology in the K-12 setting. A videodisc is about the size of an LP album. It is encoded with laser-made pits that are read back by a player which uses laser technology. Like CD-ROM, videodiscs have massive storage capacity, facilitate rapid random access, are extremely durable, and are relatively easy to use (Raleigh 1988).

Unlike CD-ROM which stores text, videodisc stores sound and images. Videodisc demonstrations will lure prospective buyers with clear images, called up from anywhere on the disc and held for indefinite periods of time without a flutter. Videotape users, who with back turned to audience have nervously searched for a particular frame only to have it jump on the screen when they did find it, will be tempted to run right out and pick up a player and discs. We must again ask ourselves the question, "Will it allow me to teach something I could not otherwise teach?" Again, software should drive the purchase of hardware since standards are not established and videodiscs tend to be hardware-specific. Prospective users need to be aware that many companies are transferring videotape and film to videodisc format which still can only be played linearly. Special microcomputer software packages are required to provide for random access. Other more specialized companies are conducting research, field-testing, and revising products in a limited number of disciplines. Some videodiscs are marketed with accompanying microcomputer software necessary to facilitate interaction. Others require authoring software to facilitate manipulation of sequence, questioning, reviewing, and tailoring its content to course objectives (Raleigh 1988).

The videodisc may well be the right medium for specific instruction. It has been highly successful in training programs where a visual medium with exacting accessibility works—teaching a specific surgical procedure in dentistry, teaching a specific welding technique, demonstrating a physics phenomenon. Teachers must understand the capability of the videodisc and be taught how to use this technology in order to maximize its capability (Hosie 1987). The videodisc is worth investigating as long as careful decision making occurs to select the right instructional application.

SOFTWARE-BASAL TEXTBOOK CONNECTIONS

Integration of the use of the computer into the existing curriculum has been a goal stated often in literature related to instructional computing (Mojkowski 1987). Textbook publishers have been reading that same literature. And so, emerging is computer software to accompany basal textbooks in a variety of disciplines (Goodspeed 1988). Is this the ultimate in integration? It depends. Much of the currently available textbook-based software is focusing on low-level tasks of recall, drill, and practice. In foreign language drill is a very important part of the learning process. When well-designed drill-and-practice software is based on the textbook, the vocabulary can match the student's vocabulary. This correlated software can be an effective aid. Such software should allow for record keeping; it should include a management system that allows students to move immediately to a level at which they need drill and not spend time drilling what they already know.

The idea of accompanying textbooks with software plays into a vulnerable market. In many school districts, boards of education have spent hundreds of thousands of dollars on computers only to find teachers and principals later asking one another, "Now that we have the machines, what shall we do with them?" The textbook-based software idea is an easy and convenient answer to that question. However, it may not always be a sound or instructionally responsible answer. Not all textbook-based software makes sense. Science textbooks that focus on process in science accompanied by software that drills on specific scientific facts do not represent good methods of integration. For, above all, the educator must make a decision about whether what the computer can do is consistent with the instructional objectives, whether it is an enhancement of the instruction, or whether it is just a way of using the computer for the sake of using the computer. Whether it is textbook-based or not may indeed be irrelevant. Instead, the questions of instructional value, content, and technical quality still apply. A question to ask in reviewing textbooks that are accompanied by software is: "Was the software designed for instructional purposes or for marketing purposes?"

NETWORKING

Hardware and software developers are fast expanding the capabilities of network systems so that data can be accessed from various locations within rooms, buildings, districts, and beyond (Lehrer 1988). Networks, at the simplest level, allow users to share peripherals such as printers. In addition, networks can allow the sharing of software and, beyond that, can provide for the sharing of data.

Sharing of resources is a popular idea as we look to the computer as a means of improving efficiency. Like any technical capability, networking will clearly have its place. Networking does have a price tag, and it is a significant factor in deciding to go to networked systems.

Still, sharing of data is a particularly powerful concept and one to be explored. Networking seems to offer the greatest benefit when we look at the computer as a tool. Sharing student data within a district, sharing personnel data between a central office and a school, and sharing files of library holdings within a district or beyond are all examples of ways to amplify the usefulness of information held on disk.

In instructional applications, networking may require very careful analysis. Some simple examples of networking are highly cost-effective and make good instructional sense. One example is to link four computers to one printer through a simple switch box so that all four students have ready access to print their files without taking out their data disk and moving to a machine equipped with a printer; most schools cannot afford the extravagance of purchasing a printer for every computer. Using a disk server or file server to share instructional software within a computer lab is another instructional application of networking. The cost-effectiveness of such an arrangement takes careful assessment since licensing agreements for using software on a networked system have price tags. How software and the specific computer lab are used must be observed carefully. Is it common for many students to use the same software at the same time regularly? How many software titles are used by whole classes sitting at computers in the lab at the same time? Does the school already own numerous "lab packs" of commonly used software? Will there be any problem with all students trying to access the server at the same time, i.e., the beginning or end of class periods?

In decision making related to networking, one must look at the cost, compare that cost with the cost of alternatives, and look at the benefit. There will be appropriate applications for networking; the issue is to determine which are most appropriate.

MASTERY MANAGEMENT SYSTEMS

Some districts are using computerized management systems funded and mandated by state legislatures. These management systems are intended to assist teachers in their decision making, communication with parents, test scoring, monitoring of student progress, and student record keeping. The idea of saving time by using scanners to score tests and generate reports is attractive to administrators as well as teachers.

However, each district needs to commit resources to inservice so that instructional objectives and test items match. Otherwise, districts fall victim to the inherent dangers of teaching to someone else's test, focusing on minimum competencies, and testing for isolated facts.

Measuring the quality of instruction is a concern for school districts, and educational literature is replete with articles related to evaluating learner outcomes. An issue to address is the question of depth versus coverage. In an age of information explosion, educators must ask whether they should focus on covering the vast quantity of current information or on developing skills to access and evaluate information. We must ask, "Do these computerized tests ask for recall of facts or do they require synthesis and evaluation?"

Indeed students do need to leave the formal school setting with some evidence of having mastered a body of knowledge. Mastery management systems can assist in affirming that mastery. However, mastery management systems cannot ensure that all students have mastered life-long learning skills. The issue of mastery management becomes the issue of what are schools intended to do for students.

PRESERVICE TEACHER TRAINING

Colleges of education have a difficult dilemma to resolve. The area of instructional computing is so recent and is evolving so rapidly that it is difficult to keep abreast of it from that vantage point. Because schools are at experimental stages in this technology, it is difficult to provide preservice teachers with sound, field-tested practices or strategies for using microcomputers effectively. Likewise, theoretical research is quite slim; there are few opportunities for field observation or controlled experimentation. Software is still emerging. Hardware is changing rapidly. All of these conditions make the task of trying to teach potential teachers about instructional computing very difficult—what should be taught?

In light of these factors, perhaps the best approach for colleges of education to take now is to develop in their students the ability to select teaching strategies and media in relation to their objectives and students. These new teachers have an array of materials, media, and strategies from which to choose. What they must learn to do is define precisely their instructional intent, consider the options, and decide how best to accomplish their task. Such instruction involves teaching these teachers-to-be about all types of media, including computers, looking at the potential uses of each and the potential strengths and weaknesses of each, setting criteria for decision making and then deciding how best to deliver instruction. Sometimes, the answer will be the microcomputer, but sometimes it will not be. A generalization for prospective teachers to make is that no medium, no technology, no strategy is right for all instructional needs.

Meanwhile, colleges of education need to be dedicating some resources to investigating the right uses of microcomputers. There need to be controlled studies of whether writing is really improved as a result of using the word processor to teach the writing process. There need to be studies of whether problem-solving strategies taught via computer transfer to other problem-solving situations. There need to be studies of the kind of information handling skills students gain by learning to manipulate data via a database management system.

One difficulty in action research is that there are still rather few computers in schools and students have rather limited access; perhaps not enough to make a measurable difference. Cleborne Maddux (1984) suggests an N-of-One strategy for research related to instructional computing at this stage of its implementation in schools. What is suggested here is that small samples may be appropriate in some studies, as opposed to the usual research concern of a large enough sample for statistical validity. This strategy may help to resolve the problem of few computers and many students in schools today.

TECHNOLOGY SPECIALIST

The emergence of microcomputer technology, with compact disc, interactive video, and other technologies close behind, creates an important staffing consideration for schools. Who will keep up with this technology? Who will follow the literature? Who will guide decision making related to what to use, when, where, and how? The need for a specialist in this area to serve schools is clear. Without such a person, vendors stand to have a great deal of input on what schools do, and they are scarcely the appropriate people to make educational decisions. In many schools, the responsibility for this area has been added to the role of the library media specialist. Whether the task goes to that person or another, someone besides the principal or the classroom teacher needs to have time available to study this area and provide leadership in decision making related to how best to use the technology, what hardware to purchase and in what quantities, how to allocate equipment within the school or district, what software to purchase, and how to use the technology effectively.

SUMMARY

Whatever issue or trend educators grow concerned about, some fundamental questions return. Those questions have to do with asking: "What do I want this instruction to accomplish?" "What options are available to me to meet that goal?" "What are the characteristics of each of those options?" "Which options have the greatest potential to match my needs?" "What must I do to implement the program?" Like any other instructional strategy or technology, instructional computing is not the answer to every question. Yet it is the right answer to some. The educator's task is to make the match between the need and the technology. It is important to see that instructional computing not be discarded because of what it cannot do, but rather is implemented fully for what it can do.

REFERENCES

Goodspeed, Jonathan. "Vendors' Summit '88: A Special Report on the Hardware Industry." *Electronic Learning* 7 (February 1988): 24–33.

Hosie, Peter. "Adopting Interactive Videodisc Technology for Education." *Educational Technology* 27 (July 1987): 5–10.

Lehrer, Ariella. "A Network Primer: Full-Fledged Educational Networks." *Classroom Computer Learning* 8 (March 1988): 37–44.

Maddux, Cleborne D. "Educational Microcomputing: The Need for Research." *Computers in the Schools* 1 (Spring 1984): 35–41.

Mojkowski, Charles. "Technology and Curriculum: Will the Promised Revolution Take Place?" *National Association of Secondary School Principals Bulletin* (February 1987): 113–18.

Raleigh, Lisa and Jennifer Brawer. "Videodisc Primer." *A+ Magazine* 6 (February 1988): 37–41.

Spitzer, Dean R. "'Megatrends in Educational Technology." *Educational Technology* 27 (September 1987): 44–47.

Vandergrift, Kay and Others. "CD-ROM: Perspectives on an Emerging Technology." *School Library Journal* 33 (June–July 1987): 27–31.

Appendices

Appendix A: Resources

In a rapidly changing area such as instructional computing, it is essential that decision makers have access to sources of current information. While this list is not exhaustive, it does represent sources of information that these authors have found to be valuable in keeping abreast of developments in the field. These are sources that assist in gathering the information for sound decision making.

PERIODICALS

Currentness is a key in technological areas. Periodical literature offers the best print medium for recent developments in the field. Certain periodicals are particularly useful in the K-12 setting. Those periodicals have been listed here.

A+ Magazine. Ziff Davis, One Park Avenue, New York, NY 10016.
Current information on hardware and software in general personal computer use. Frequent articles related to educational computing.

Classroom Computer Learning. 19 Davis Drive, Belmont, CA 94002.
Intended audience is classroom teachers, computer coordinators, and library media professionals. Information on recent developments in hardware as well as ideas on the use of software and software reviews.

The Computing Teacher. ICCE, University of Oregon, 1787 Agate Street, Eugene, OR 97403-1923.
Intended audience is K-12 teachers and administrators. Contains articles for both the researcher and the practitioner.

Educational Technology. 140 Sylvan Avenue, Engelwood Cliffs, NJ 07632.
Intended audience is decision makers. Contains articles related to applied research.

Tech Trends. AECT, 1126 16th Street N.W., Washington, DC 20036.
Intended audience is educational technology specialists. Contains articles on hardware and planning for instructional uses of technology.

SOFTWARE REVIEWS

Software selection is a difficult process. This process can begin with the examination of software reviews. While previewing software is the best way to make a match with the instructional needs, published reviews can provide a starting point for the sifting process. The reviewing sources listed below contain critical, rather than merely descriptive, reviews. As one reads reviews, it is important to determine the philosophical perspective of the reviewer and/or the publication. It is important to remember that highly acclaimed software may or may not be right for your instructional setting. It is, in the end, the match between your school's needs and the software that is the goal.

Classroom Computer Learning. 19 Davis Drive, Belmont, CA 94002.

The Computing Teacher. ICCE, University of Oregon, 1787 Agate Street, Eugene, OR 97403-1923.

Educational Technology. 140 Sylvan Avenue, Engelwood Cliffs, NJ 07632.

Electronic Learning. 730 Broadway, New York, NY 10003.

MicroSIFT Courseware Evaluation. Northwest Regional Educational Laboratory, 300 SW 6th Avenue, Portland, OR 97204.

In addition to general publications in the educational technology field, journals of professional associations in various disciplines tend to carry reviews of software related to the content area. Examples include *Social Education, Arithmetic Teacher, Science and Children,* and *School Science and Mathematics.*

For retrospective purchasing or descriptions of software available by subject, the curriculum software guides published by Apple Computer Inc. are useful. Guides are available for language arts, mathematics, and science.

CONFERENCES

Meetings of state and national associations provide valuable opportunities for learning about new developments and studies and for meeting people who share interests and concerns.

COMMTEX. International Communications Industries Association, 3150 Spring Street, Fairfax, VA 22031-2399.
Annual in the winter.

National Educational Computing Conference. Sponsored by the International Council for Computers in Education, University of Oregon, 1787 Agate Street, Eugene, OR 97403-1923.
Annual in the summer.

HUMAN RESOURCES

Perhaps one of the most difficult, yet most valuable, sources to locate is people. This list of human resources includes just a few of the outstanding educators working in the area of instructional computing. These are people with whom the authors have had firsthand experience, either by hearing them present at conferences, corresponding with them, or seeing in action programs for which they are responsible. While we can acknowledge that there are many more, these people may provide readers with the beginnings of a network. In arranging speakers for conferences, seeking answers to questions, or seeking consultation to one's district or school, these people may be able to provide some answers.

Billings, Karen. *Topic:* Evaluating Computer Education Programs. Logo Computer Systems, 555 W. 57th St., New York, NY 10102.

Cory, Sheila. *Topic:* Evaluating Computer Education Programs. Chapel-Hill-Carborro City Schools, Merritt Mill Rd., Chapel Hill, NC 27514.

Epler, Doris. *Topic:* Information Access. Department of Education, Harrisburg, PA 17105.

Moursund, David. *Topic:* District Planning for Instructional Computing. International Council for Computers in Education, 1787 Agate St. Eugene, OR 97403.

O'Brien, Thomas. *Topic:* Teaching Problem Solving Using the Computer. Teachers' Center Project, Southern Illinois University, Edwardsville, IL 62026.

Pogrow, Stanley. *Topic:* Teaching Thinking Skills Using the Computer. University of Arizona, P.O. Box 22801, Tucson, AZ 85706.

Schiffman, Shirl. *Topic:* Integrating Computing and Curriculum. 723 Watermark Pl., Columbia, SC 29210.

Stoeker, John. *Topic:* Keyboarding Instruction. University of Oregon, 4105 Oak St., Eugene, OR 97405.

van Deusen, Robert Moon. *Topic:* Teaching Thinking Skills Using the Computer. Grant Wood Area Education Agency, Cedar Rapids, IA 52404.

Wresch, William. *Topic:* Teaching the Writing Process Using the Computer. Dept. of Mathematics and Computing, University of Wisconsin, Stevens Point, WI 54481.

Appendix B: Software Producers

The following companies produce software that has been cited or described in this book:

Activision, Inc., 2350 Bayshore Pkwy., Mountain View, CA 94043

Aldus Corporation, 411 First Ave., Suite 200, Seattle, WA 98104

Apple Computer, Inc., 20515 Mariani Ave., Cupertino, CA 95014

Broderbund Software, 17 Paul Dr., San Rafael, CA 94903

BRS, 1200 Route 7, Latham, NY 12110

CONDUIT, University of Iowa, Oakdale Campus, Iowa City, IA 52242

C.U.E. SoftSwap, P.O. Box 271704, Concord, CA 94527-1704

Dialog Information Services, Inc., 3460 Hillview Ave., Palo Alto, CA 94304

Educational Activities, 1937 Grand Ave., Baldwin, NY 11520

Educational Technology Center, Harvard Graduate School, 337 Guttman Library, Appian Way, Cambridge, MA 02138

Electronic Arts, 1820 Gateway Dr., San Mateo, CA 94404

Follett Software Co., 4506 Northwest Hwy., Crystal Lake, IL 60014

Holt, Rinehart & Winston, 6277 Sea Harbor Dr., Orlando, FL 32821

HRM Software, 175 Tompkins Ave., Pleasantville, NY 10570

H.W. Wilson Company, 950 University Ave., Bronx, NY 10452

Kitchen Sink Software, 903 Knebworth Ct., Westerville, OH 45081

Learning Company, P.O. Box 2168, Menlo Park, CA 94025

Letraset, 40 Eisenhower Dr., Paramus, NJ 07652

Lotus Development Corporation, 55 Cambridge Pkwy., Cambridge, MA 02142

McGraw-Hill, 13955 Manchester Rd., Manchester, MO 63011

Microsoft Corporation, 10700 Northup Way, Bellevue, WA 98004

Miliken Publishing Co., 1100 Research Blvd., Box 21579, St. Louis, MO 63132

Minnesota Educational Computing Consortium, 3490 Lexington Ave., North, St. Paul, MN 55126

Scholastic, Inc., 2931 E. McCarty St., Box 7503, Jefferson City, MO 65102

Sensible Software, Inc., 335 E. Big Beaver Rd., Troy, MI 48084

Silicon Beach, P.O. Box 261430, San Diego, CA 92126

South Western Publishing Co., 5101 Madison Rd., Cincinnati, OH 45227

Springboard Software, Inc., 7807 Creekridge Circle, Minneapolis, MN 55435

Sunburst Communication, 39 Washington Ave., Pleasantville, NY 10570

Terrapin, Inc., 222 Third St., Cambridge, MA 02142

Tom Snyder Productions, 90 Sherman St., Cambridge, MA 02140

Versacad Corporation, 2124 Main St., Huntington Beach, CA 92468

Index

Compiled by Linda Webster

Note: Initial-capitalized terms that appear in roman typeface indicate databases or software programs.

Mary Jo Langhorne is Library Media Specialist, Northwest Junior High School, Iowa City Community Schools, Iowa City, Iowa.

Jean O. Donham is District Library Media Coordinator, Iowa City Community Schools, Iowa City, Iowa.

June F. Gross is Library Media Specialist, St. Louis Park Junior High School, St. Louis Park, Minnesota.

Denise Rehmke is Library Media Specialist, South East Junior High School, Iowa City Community Schools, Iowa City, Iowa.